RADICAL: sweeping, complete
Essential
relentless,
total,
absolute.
Unconditional
profound,
revolutionary,
far-reaching.

FORGIVENESS: to grant relief
Releasing
liberate,
absolve,
provide sanctuary.
Redemptive
pardon,
rescue,
set free.

What Real Women Say
about Julie Ann Barnhill, her books, and her workshops . . .

There wasn't a page in this book that didn't have "ME" written all over it.

Thank you for writing such a hilarious, yet frank book about the wonder of God's AMAZING grace. You've exposed your life and experiences so that others may see how scandalous God's grace is! I can't wait to read *Radical Forgiveness*—I really need it!

I am a "new" Christian. I've often felt overwhelmed with the daunting task of *becoming* a Christian mom, wife, friend, employee. . . . Your simple and laugh-out-loud instruction has given me hope.

Even though I was raised in the church, I've made some very bad choices. It's a good thing God's grace is in never-ending supply, 'cuz I sure have used quite a bit of it! Thank you for showing me how to give those things to the cross and allow scandalous grace to take care of the rest!

For the first time in 53 years I'm admitting my scorched places. I had them all along and just didn't recognize them . . . or how they were affecting my life and relationships. Thanks a bunch— from the bottom of my heart!

You have a special way about you. . . . Your humor and energy grabbed my attention.

Thank you for your words, your light, your salt, your life, and your passion.

Three years ago, when I was 37, I found out my dad was not my biological father. My mom was raped by someone she knew. When you talked about the boy and the *A* on his forehead, and how he is the reminder of sin, that is how I have felt—only I have an *R* for product of Rape . . . and a reminder of a painful time for my mother. I know that God turns ugly situations into beautiful blessings, but some days I require more grace than others. I will continue to pray about it, but in the meantime your message reinforced to me that God is the only Father I truly need.

I can relate to everything you said. I am 41 years old and have just recently let go of comparing myself with others.

I have been in therapy for 13 years because of my scorched places. I came to hear you with a broken heart, but left with hope.

Thank you for being candid. I'm 23 and getting married in September. I don't even like to read, but God put this book in my hand for a reason—because I needed to learn how to accept myself. I'll probably be the same weight and have the same acne as I do now for the rest of my life, but now I realize that's not even important.

I've always been insecure, and lately I've gained a lot of weight. This makes me feel even worse about myself. Thank you for showing me how to stop comparing myself to others.

I have never felt like I was what God wanted—like I was a very good Christian. When you said God accepts us even with our mistakes and faults, a warm feeling of peace came over me. I wanted to run up and give you a great big hug!

Until *Scandalous Grace,* I really never believed that other women thought the things that I did. I thought I was the only one who weighed herself every day.

I am a single mother of 2 wonderful girls, ages 11 and 7. And yet it is like you have lived my life in parts . . . as if I were writing the book myself! It is so wonderful to know that I am "normal."

You are hilarious, yet you touch the secret places of my mind and my heart. You have made my entire life better!

You've given me permission to accept myself, while not making excuses for attitudes and behavior that are destructive.

I've been a "mess" more times than I care to remember. Sometimes that makes it hard to believe God still loves me. But instead of rolling my eyes at another "God loves you" book, you had me hooked from the first page!

I can't tell you how liberating it is to find out that there are so many other women out there just like me. Only the addresses change! More liberating still is to know that God's grace and his radical forgiveness is sufficient.

I've read lots of self-help books, but none of them impacted my life like your workshop.

You have *got* to get your own talk show! I have never laughed so hard in my life! Thank you for a wonderful, wonderful time!

Talk about a timely, appropriate message for me and my friends. You just keep on doin' what you're doin', girlfriend!

OTHER BOOKS
BY JULIE ANN BARNHILL

Scandalous Grace

She's Gonna Blow! Real Help for Moms Dealing with Anger

She's Gonna Blow! CD Audio Abridgment
Read by the Author

'Til Debt Do Us Part

Radical Forgiveness

It's time to wipe your
slate clean!

JULIE ANN
BARNHILL

TYNDALE HOUSE PUBLISHERS, INC.
WHEATON, ILLINOIS

Visit Tyndale's exciting Web site at www.tyndale.com

Published in association with the literary agency of Alive Communications, Inc., 7680 Goddard Street, Suite 200, Colorado Springs, CO 80920.

Edited by Ramona Cramer Tucker

Designed by Luke Daab

Library of Congress Cataloging-in-Publication Data

Barnhill, Julie Ann, date.
  Radical forgiveness : it's time to wipe your slate clean! / Julie Ann Barnhill.
    p. cm.
  Includes bibliographical references.
  ISBN 1-4143-0031-X (pbk.)
  1. Forgiveness—Religious aspects—Christianity. I. Title.
  BV4647.F55B37 2004
  234'.5—dc22   2004017232

Printed in the United States of America

10 09 08 07 06 05 04
7 6 5 4 3 2 1

To my daughter, Kristen

My, how time has flown . . .

From whispered lullabies sung sweet and low,

to CD marathons of Norah Jones.

Taking your first steps at eight months and letting go,

Now it's car keys that you hold.

You are my firstborn,

my only girl,

A one-of-a-kind creation with dancing eyes

and a head full of curls.

As you navigate your way through womanhood and faith,

Joys and sorrow,

Gain and loss,

Know these two things remain . . .

He is faithful

and

I love you, sweet girl.

Always,

Forever,

Mom

Contents

Acknowledgments ✳ **xiii**

1. Give It the Old Hanky Wave! ✳ **1**

2. A Mess of Magnificent Proportions ✳ **9**

3. I've Never Told This to Anyone . . . ✳ **25**

4. Déjà Vu . . . All Over Again ✳ **39**

5. It's All about Me ✳ **53**

6. Trading Spaces ✳ **67**

7. I Would If I Could . . . But I Can't, So I Won't ✳ **81**

8. Infinity + 1 ✳ **95**

9. Forgive and Forget? . . . and Other Myths ✳ **107**

10. Girlfriend 9-1-1! ✳ **125**

11. Falling Forward ✳ **139**

12. Wide-Open Spaces ✳ **151**

Forgiveness Observed ✳ **159**

A Radical Recipe ✳ **165**

About the Author ✳ **167**

Endnotes ✳ **169**

Acknowledgments

Ramona Cramer Tucker: Editor and friend, an extraordinary gift from God. You have summed up scandalous grace and radical forgiveness in this glorious process of writing and ministry. Now onward to the exquisite hope of future books and ideas!

Karen Watson and Carol Traver: Thanks for holding my author hand during the four-hour minibreakdown session in February 2004. Who knew writing could be so, well, hard? (Smile!) You both possess an incredible talent for making me laugh, understanding my I've-got-a-shotgun-vision-idea-for-this-book-and-chapter thoughts, and hearing my heart as a woman, a friend, and a writer.

The fa-boo staff of marketing, publicity, and author relations at Tyndale Publishing: Mavis, Jill, Jacki, Linda, Keri, Travis—I couldn't be doing this without you wonderful, nutty, group of women (and man!). Your creative thinking astounds me and the fact that you ALL either make me laugh so hard I snort or do the same around me, makes me love you even more. Here's to more desert-laden marketing extravaganzas and red-hued gag gifts!

My children—Kristen, Ricky, and Patrick: You have been divine instruments of instruction in my life. I love you beyond measure, treasure your company, and revel in the fact that we are not only mother and children, but sisters and brothers through Jesus Christ.

Rick: You'll be on every acknowledgment page I write. Once again, you have allowed me to pursue the desire of my heart—writing and speaking—and have managed to keep the household going as I mutter and type, rant and rejoice in my humble writing "bat cave."

Chip MacGregor: A couple of years ago you brought my name to the attention of editors at Tyndale House Publishers. I believe I was in bed sick with the flu when you called and left a message on my voice mail saying, "While you were eating bonbons in Illinois, I was ONLY talking to one of the largest publishing houses about your potential and your writing voice." I called you back and made a small comment about your being crazy and wondering what my "voice" was exactly. But alas, here we are, two books down the road with more in sight. Thank you for believing in me, Chip, and helping to make this magnificent relationship with Tyndale possible.

Gracie Malone and Cynthia Spell Humbert: You never told me to shut up. Not after a hundred phone calls and a thousand e-mails lamenting my inability to think and write. You know many of the places I've needed radical rescue, for you have been the life preservers I've held tightly to. I love you, friends.

And everyone who has ever put up with me and forgiven me time and time again. Hmm, that would pretty much cover the entire free world!

To forgive is to put down your 50-pound pack
after a 10-mile climb up a mountain.
To forgive is to fall into a chair after a 15-mile marathon.
To forgive is to set a prisoner free
and discover that the prisoner was you.
To forgive is to reach back into your hurting past
and recreate it in your memory so that you can begin again.
To forgive is to dance to the beat of God's forgiving heart.
It is to ride the crest of love's strongest wave.[1]
Lewis B. Smedes

This is the journey of radical forgiveness, radical redemption, radical and purposeful living. . . .

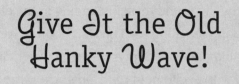

1
Give It the Old Hanky Wave!

It's hard to believe another year and writing deadline has passed since we first got acquainted in *Scandalous Grace.*

While we've been apart, I've attempted to make further peace with "The Poodge" (i.e. the lower portion of the abdomen that refuses to lie down, mind its own business, and go away) by purchasing the books and products of Bill Phillips' *Body for Life,* Atkins Diet Plus! Medifast liquid drink, as well as a two-month stint with Weight Watchers. I was doing okay until those pesky holiday seasons arrived *(Easter, Thanksgiving, Ground-hog Day, the entire month of December),* and as a result I ended with a final net loss of .2 pounds and nearly $600 from the old checkbook register.

During the same period of time, I contemplated digesting a dietary supplement endorsed by notorious model-reality tele-vision diva, Anna Nicole Smith. I was reading through a *People* magazine while standing in the checkout lane of Target when I came across a two-page photo insert of said diva. Gasping in alarm *(note: Anna was fully clothed)* I was taken aback by her claim of having lost more than 55 pounds with the help of the nutritional supplement TrimSpa. Immediately I wanted the answer to one question and one question only: Where do I buy TrimSpa?!

Quickly enough I found myself standing in the diet aid aisle of Walgreens and reaching for The Holy Grail of weight loss potential. I could almost feel myself losing weight just holding the jar. Giddy with excitement *(and fantasies of size 4 clothes shopping),* I began to scan the ingredients list. Most of it read like an unknown language with the exception of a bold disclaimer at the bottom of the bottle:

Warning: If you are allergic to shellfish, please consult your physician before taking this product.

Well, it figures I'd find myself on the cusp of weight loss nirvana, only to have it snatched from my chubby grasp! But then I considered buying it anyway. After all, I tried to tell myself, it isn't like I have a *serious* allergy to shellfish. Nah . . . all a little shrimp does to my system is puff it up like a blowfish, constrict my airway, and raise hives the color of purple Kool-Aid everywhere on my body.

Hello?!!

Sometimes my ability to *not* think at age 38 astounds even me.

So here we are again: chick to chick, author to reader, and most importantly, girlfriend to girlfriend. I thought it wise—given the time since we last spoke—to kick off our time with another round of hanky wave truth.

For those new to the ranks allow me to give a brief explanation.

While speaking to women nationally and internationally, I've discovered that many audiences assume speakers somehow live above the fray of real life. Perhaps it has something to do with our standing on a platform, holding a microphone, or being able to get ready that morning in a hotel room with few, if any, distractions. Whatever the case may be, more than one woman has shared with me her preconceived notions of speakers having it all together and managing to do so with seemingly perfect smiles, perfect bodies, perfect families, and perfect stories of success. (It's important to note that women believed such things *prior* to meeting *me*.) Well, I think God has personally put me on this earth to blow that whole image to smithereens. Just ask my husband, my kids, or check out my thighs!

Everyone needs help along the journey of life because nobody has life "all figured out." All of us have our areas in which we thrive, and areas in which we just survive, sometimes only barely. But by walking down the path together, we can figure it out—and have a lot more fun. And that's just what hanky wave truth brings—fun among women by creating a connection between myself, the readers of this book or my audience when I speak, as well as individual participants seated (or reading) near one another.

I've found the most effective and laugh-out-loud enjoyable manner of accomplishing this is through the use of a linen hanky and a few snappy, slightly dysfunctional, and estrogen-laced observations and comments. Observations you can agree or commiserate with—and then, of course, show your female support by wildly waving a hanky back. Of course, one is not limited to a mere hanky for the wild waving. Feel free to grab a Kleenex, diaper wipe, stretched-out bra, or a crumpled receipt from your last credit card purchase. It really doesn't matter the type of hanky as long as your hand and attitude are attached to it, and you're ready to wave.

So, without further ado—grab a hanky or faux stand-in, assume "the position,"* and prepare to identify as tens of thousands of fabulous chicks before you have!

✳ If you believe all forms of cosmetic surgery should be covered by any and all insurance policies under a deductible co-pay of $10—give me a hanky wave.

✳ If you've ever one-handedly removed your bra while driving five miles over the speed limit and never lost your lane—give me a hanky wave.

✳ If you've ever bought a pair of painful shoes just because they made your calves look fabulous—give me a hanky wave.

✳ If you've ever quoted the Real Woman Bad Food Motto, "I made this food, you will eat this food, and I don't care how bad you think it tastes"—give me a hanky wave.

✳ If you understand the medicinal power of chocolate in that it makes you "feel better"—give me a hanky wave.

✳ If you've ever watched a beautiful woman walk into a room and said to yourself, *Yep, I hate her*—give me a hanky wave.

✳ If you have ever wanted to slam into the back end of the

* Standing, knees slightly bent, hand on one hip, hanky prepared for takeoff in the other! (For a more colorful "attitude" description, refer to page 2 of *Scandalous Grace.*)

car in front of you just because the following sticker was attached to their bumper—"Proud Parent of an A+ Honor Student"—give me a hanky wave.

✳ If you'd like to purchase a bumper sticker that reads, "Stressed Parent of a C- (Barely) Student"—give me a hanky wave.

✳ If you have discovered that kneecaps, as well as breasts, can droop and go off course—give me a hanky wave.

✳ If you ever told someone you forgive them but crossed your fingers behind your back while doing so (and you were over 30 when you did it!)—give me a hanky wave.

✳ If you know how to spell *forgiveness* but sometimes don't feel like you have a clue what it *really* means—give me a hanky wave.

Whoo-ha! It seems the more things change, the more they stay the same.

You have once again officially entered the Real Woman Reading Zone. And for the next few hours, days, or weeks *(hey, we women all have multiple interruptions, so no guilt!)* it takes to read this book, I want you to have your own "Girls Night Out."

But you have to do something first. Lose any and all forms of body shapers or bras *(yes, you read me right)*. I want you to throw off any and all encumbering straps or confining stretches of spandex. Let your body breathe, woman! Then find your most comfortable spot. Jump back into bed, run some bath-water, or sit in your favorite chair. Whatever the place . . . just get there. And once you're finally settled, read.

Read and laugh.

Read and cry.

Read and sigh.

Read and say aloud, "That is so me!"

In *Radical Forgiveness,* we're going to talk about . . . well, forgiveness. Not "Forgiveness in 5 Easy Steps"—because there is no such thing. Anyone who sells you a "light and easy" forgiveness is really selling something worthless, for it certainly won't last.

Instead we're going to talk about what it *really* means to forgive those who have hurt you, to forgive yourself for the dumb things you've done, and to forgive God for what he has— or hasn't—done in your life.

Along the way I'll reveal some of the areas I struggle with— not so you can see how bad or good of a person I am, but because we are fellow travelers on the road.

What does true forgiveness have to do with your "here and now"? And why is it so important? Even more, is getting over the forgiveness hump really worth all the work *(groan)*?

Radical, cleansing forgiveness means walking away from sin, shame, fear, and disappointment. It means facing each day with a lighter burden, a lighter heart, and a new purpose to look ahead. *(Turn back to the beginning of this chapter and reread the quote by Lewis B. Smedes. Wouldn't you like to feel that way every day?)*

God is calling you to a life of freedom—to a life that's radically redeemed by his truth. A life that isn't perfect, because no life is perfect on this earth. But a life in which you can be released of everything that weighs you down and live daily in the light of a forgiveness that is so total, so profound, so sweeping, and so satisfying that you will be radically changed! Right here and right now you can have a new zest for life, a new hope for the future, and a new and radical freedom!

Radically His,
Julie Ann Barnhill

2

A Mess of Magnificent Proportions

Hi. My name is Julie, and I am a mess.

For most of my 38 years I've found myself to be in said state. This bit of messaholic truth isn't altogether shocking, once you take a few facts into consideration.

Fact: I routinely forget how particular letters of the alphabet are composed when signing checks or attempting to write my own name—thereby leaving me no other option than to scrawl random lines and dashes in a mad attempt to form the letters *J* and *B*.

Fact: I'm prone to forget any and all manner of pertinent information when attempting to think and speak at the same time. Sigh. This has happened more times than I care to—or can even—recall. Such as the night I was about to wrap up a spectacular keynote presentation. The audience had been a speaker's dream. They laughed *(and snorted)* in all the right places.

Then, just as I was about to wrap it all up with a knock-their-socks-off finale . . . it happened.

Right there, smack-dab midsentence, I utterly and completely forgot my final point. I'm talking biblical "as far as the east is

from the west" forgotten. I had no clue where I was going or
where I had been.

Phfft.

Brain drain.

Nobody was home.

Looking into the crowd I queried, "What was my last point?"

Everyone laughed. *Isn't she clever?* they thought perhaps.

"No really," I pleaded. "Was anyone taking notes?"

Fact: When barking out parental decrees I routinely forget
the names of my own children, hence randomly spouting
names of their siblings, nephews, and even annoying animated
cartoon characters when attempting to gain their attention.*

I'm a mess all right.

✳ ✳ ✳

Take the time I traveled to Chicago, for instance. I was to
attend a Thursday evening business dinner, spend the night at
a local bed-and-breakfast, and then drive to Midway Airport
the following morning to board a plane for Fraser, Michigan.
Thankfully a light dusting of snow that Friday morning did not
impede busy Chicago traffic, and I found myself pulling into the
long-term budget parking lot a couple of hours ahead of schedule. That was a good thing, for having failed to consider the
walking distance to the nearest airport shuttle pickup, I found
myself wandering aimlessly through the Red and Blue economy
parking lot maze—haphazardly wheeling an oversized chunk
of luggage behind me.

---

* "Ricky! No, I mean Brett! Doh! . . . BART! You know who you are! Now stop
annoying your brother!"

I lost a few minutes at the metal detector *(Tip: Do not wear underwire)*. Upon verification that my reinforced bustline and I posed no immediate threat to national security, I made my way down Concourse B, found my gate area, and plunked myself in front of the continuous *(and may I add droning)* news coverage of CNN. Inhaling the only breakfast item available for purchase *(Global Coast chili-and-cheese hot dog)*, I began to review the day's itinerary.

The scheduled flight departure was set for 11:28 A.M., with an estimated arrival at Detroit International Airport of 12:34 P.M. I was to be picked up by the event meeting planner and driven to my hotel, where I would then spend the remainder of the day relaxing in my room, reading a book or two, joining a few women from the area for supper, and preparing for Saturday morning's conference.

Ah, nothing but blue skies did I see.

Um, make that blue skies minus takeoff.

Moments after taxiing from our gate, the steely voice of the flight captain announced, "Ladies and gentlemen, we have a slight mechanical problem. It appears one of our jet engines is being a bit cranky today and is refusing to engage. We're going to make our way back to the terminal and take care of this minor inconvenience as soon as possible."

Disgruntled murmurings trickled through coach seating as I turned to both 12E and 12D seatmates and inquired, "Did he just say a slight mechanical problem with an engine?"

Call me crazy, but I believe there are certain five word phrases that shouldn't be spoken by certain people:

DOCTORS: Let's keep our fingers crossed.

TODDLERS: I did it all myself.

SALESCLERKS: Your card has been denied.

ADULT PARENTS: We're spending our kid's inheritance.

JET CAPTAINS: Slight mechanical problem with engine.

Do any of the above ever bode well for the listening audience? I think not.

Call me a stickler for semantics, but in my "I'd rather not plummet 28,000 feet to earth" thesaurus of life there isn't a "slight" *anything* on a 144,000-pound tube of steel hurtling through the atmosphere. Or taxiing back to Gate 15 at 3 mph.

Relieved we would not be tempting atmospheric reality, I listened and then decoded the Friendly Skies Corporate disclaimer being read by our flight attendant.

What I heard: "Ladies and gentlemen, due to a slight mechanical problem, we are asking you to disembark. Please take all carry-on items off the jet as you leave, and be sure to remain in the gate area until proper corrections have been made. Unfortunately, the part needed for this engine is not stocked in our Chicago garage. It will, however, arrive from our Detroit office within an anticipated period of six to seven hours. Thank you for flying One Cosmos Airlines."

What she really wanted to say: "Ladies and gentlemen, our anticipated time of departure is really anyone's guess. You see it depends on a lot of stuff, like actually getting that part here from Detroit. That's going to be extremely iffy. It can only be replaced by union-certified mechanics—mechanics who, at this very moment, are seriously considering striking. Come on—do you really think you're going to get out of here today? Get real! In all likelihood you'll be forced, by circumstances within our control, to eat really bad Mexican food at the restaurant down the concourse and then to suffer equal parts indigestion and indignation amongst the complete strangers standing around you. And by the way, we saw that look in your eye when you were disembarking. Don't even think about approaching the desk and asking for a travel voucher. We don't do vouchers. Just face facts. You have a snowball's chance in Tahiti of making it to Detroit in this, your earthly lifetime. Thank you for flying One Cosmos Airlines."

Now, I'd like to tell you I calmly and matter-of-factly dealt with this minor glitch in a composed, seasoned-traveler kind of way. That I thought out all options in a reasonable and adultlike fashion. But, hey, I think you know different. I did, in fact, panic. My inner dialogue went something like this *(for best results, read fast)*:

What am I going to do?

How am I ever going to manage to get to Detroit, meet the ladies, have dinner, and be rested for tomorrow's event?

Let's see . . . maybe I could fly on another airplane (quick beeline to nearest customer service desk—not a chance).

Maybe I could fly out extra early Saturday morning and still make it (quick check of flight schedules—not a chance).

Oh, this is just great! I guess I'm going to have to drive to Detroit (quick check with the traveler seated nearby—it'll be a good five- to six-hour drive).

Well, that's just great. I'm going to have to rent a car, drive the entire distance alone, and get in after midnight!

But wait . . . (quickly check wallet, discover I'm traveling with my low-credit-line MasterCard). Did I pay this credit card bill online yesterday? If I didn't, I am so toast. I won't have enough credit for the rental. Why didn't I pay that stupid bill?. . .

Since my meltdown was going full throttle, it seemed like a wonderful time to get my husband in on things. I dialed home on my cell phone and started in as soon as Rick picked up.

Our conversation went something like this:

"Hello."

Without even taking a breath, I blurted out, "Do you remember if I paid the MasterCard online this week?"

"Uh, I'm assuming I'm talking to my lovely wife, Julie?"

"Yeah, yeah, yeah, it's me—look, do you remember if I paid that bill or not?"

"Sorry, I don't. Would you like me to check online for you?"

"Yeah, do that . . ."

Then Rick's voice turned puzzled. "Why are you worried about the credit card balance anyway? Didn't you take your new platinum business card with the higher credit limit?"

"No," I said sarcastically. "I left that one at home on the desk and now a stupid engine on our stupid jet quit working and it's going to be at least six to seven hours before it's fixed and the airline isn't making any promises that we'll actually be able to fly out tonight and I have to get to Detroit because it's pretty tacky not to show up as a keynote speaker and if I don't rent a car and drive over there I don't know how I'm going to get there and—"*

Rick attempted to interject. "Ju—"

---

* I speak without commas when engaged in a full-blown meltdown.

Deftly avoiding his attempt, I resumed my spiel.* "And if I didn't pay that credit card bill, I probably don't have enough credit to rent a car and I am such an idiot for leaving my business card on the desk. . . ."

"Juli—" he attempted again.

" . . . but you know what? Now that you've got me thinking about it, I probably should only purchase a one-way rental because I'll still have my ticket for the flight back. No, that won't work, because my ticket will be cancelled if I don't use the first portion of it. . . . "

Finally the man could take it no longer.

This time he flat out interrupted and shouted, "Julie, would you please shut up for one minute and listen to me?!"

Then I, being the submissive wife I am, closed my mouth, lowered my eyes, and muttered under my breath, "This had better be good."

Clearing his throat and, with just the slightest hint of a smile tucked between his words, Rick spoke. "Okay, babe, I'm going to say this very slowly, and I want you to hear every word. You . . . drove . . . your . . . car . . . to . . . the . . . airport . . . this . . . morning."

"Well, I'll be," I exclaimed and proceeded to bang my head against the nearest roasted almond kiosk.

✳ ✳ ✳

I think you're going to click with more than a few things in the following pages because, despite fleeting moments of

---

* I love a great drama.

15-minute fame with Oprah, Dick Clark, and Dr. James Dobson, my life isn't all together—not by a long shot.

There are relationships that aren't quite what they should be, and most, if not all, of the blame can be placed on me. There are specific temptations, grudges, vices, and selfish motives I know in my head and heart are wrong, yet I find myself succumbing to them time and time again. And there are flat out sins I have willfully chosen to commit, despite the fact they go against the very faith I claim to possess as a believer.

How crazy is that? As crazy as admitting it, perhaps!

Can you relate?

I'm thinking you can.

For once again I find myself writing not only out of my struggle but from the comments, confessions, and conversations drawn from thousands of women I have met personally or communicated with via e-mail. For better or worse, it seems we have all fallen short in our relationships with others and God—not to mention how we fall short in the ways we treat ourselves.

All of us need to embrace the messy reality of our existence, for nothing can happen until we fully admit it.

But there are a few prerequisites for all of us.

> #1: We must come just as we are.
> #2: We must bring all our messes—no attempting to dress them up or shove them in a laundry basket and hide them away.
> #3: We can't compare our mess to anyone else's.

#4: And most important, we must confess with our own
      mouth the reality of our situation.
Are you ready?

✳ ✳ ✳

I tell you what—since this was my idea to begin with, I'll go first.

(Ahem)

"I am a mess."

There—I said it.

Now it's your turn.

Don't be shy.

No whispering!

Just say it.

Confess it.

Throw aside control issues or perfectionist tendencies and just do it.

Admit once and for all that you don't have it all together.

"I am a mess."

While you're confessing, I'd like to submit this additional fact regarding my own messy reality. I am a woman who knows only one manner in which to engage life—all or nothing.

It's true. I will either be captivated utterly and completely by something . . . or have no interest in it whatsoever for the remainder of my life on earth.

Twenty-six years ago I picked out the china pattern I wanted to set my table with as an adult. Just this Christmas I lovingly placed six settings of Gorham, Kingsbury, around the dining room table and thought, *I like this as much as I did when I was 12 years old.*

All or nothing.

Translated into real woman terms, that means I will attempt to lose 15 pounds in two days *(and believe all the while it is possible)*, or I will eat my way through 15 pounds of Hostess chocolate HoHos instead.

All or nothing.

Relationally, I have a strong tendency to move at warp speed—often scaring the daylights out of more snail-prone strangers and tentative acquaintances. *(James Bond wishes he had a car that accelerated at Julie-speed)*.

All or nothing.

And regarding the spiritual areas of my life? Well, I've attended rowdy women's retreats and stayed up all night discussing pre-destination, the second coming of Jesus, and the writings of Dr. Francis Schaeffer. I've also fallen asleep while praying.

Therefore, ladies, in keeping with my all-or-nothing tendencies, I proclaim I am not just a mess—*I am a mess of magnificent proportions.*

And yes, I'd like you to embrace and confess this magnificent truth until it rolls comfortably off your tongue. Go ahead, try it a time or two!

I
Am
A
Mess
Of
Magnificent (dramatic arm movements strongly encouraged)
Proportions

Now, if we were all sitting side by side, or shoulder to shoulder, I'd ask you to look another woman directly in the eye, smile sweetly, and say to her, "You are a mess." Trust me, you would love it.

So do the next best thing: In the next few minutes or hours grab your teenage daughter, sister, favorite aunt, best friend, mother—anyone female—and make that declaration. *(Feel free to explain yourself a bit afterwards and give them a big hug as well!)*

I believe there are two important reasons why we need to make this seven-word confession.

First, it succeeds in placing all of us on the same living field. The totem pole of perceived spiritual hierarchy is gloriously toppled once you hear an author, speaker, friend, or—gasp— even a pastor, declare their messiness. Publicly confessing our sins and foibles to one another is one of the prime ingredients for experiencing a whole and healthy life.[1]

Second, it jump-starts our journey toward radical forgiveness—toward our discovering and embracing divine redemption, which heals us from our messes, rescues us from the power of our past, and frees us from the penalties and punishments chalked up by our misdeeds.[2]

I submit that far too many women along the road of faith have allowed themselves to believe their individual sins are greater, deeper, and uglier, than anyone else's—thereby rendering them exempt from God's divine, essential, absolute, complete, relentless, and radical ability and authority to redeem— to forgive. And as a result we have talked *around* the subject of those sins—admitting rather to a lightweight cotton-candy list of problems.

We have chosen to pretend everything is okay rather than admit our mess. In fact, we've become so adept at deflecting our need for a savior from that mess that oftentimes we appear just like that—saints without a savior.

I wish you could see the look on the faces and hear the responses from the women who declare, "I am a mess" in conference and retreat settings. After an initial wave of nervous laughter and twitchy eye movements, a raucous roar always follows, accompanied by the electrified buzz of conversation as women let down their guard and discover they are not alone.

You have insecurities?

Me too.

You have made colossal mistakes even when you knew better?

Ditto.

You've been hurt by someone and have found it difficult— if not impossible—to forgive?

Ditto again.

You have questioned or even despised God's timing and unnerving silence and felt unbearable guilt while doing so?

Others have been there too.

You have vowed to stop doing, or saying, or believing, or holding onto that certain thing or habit or person? And then found yourself doing, saying, believing, or holding onto that thing, habit, or person, a short time later?

Well, welcome to the world of XX chromosomes, free will, sin, and girlfriend honesty.

Look, we've all toyed with sin—carelessly believing it was

something we could outwit or out-quit—only to find ourselves held hostage emotionally, mentally, spiritually, or sexually, to its addicting power.

All of us—author, reader, girlfriend, and stranger alike—are in need of a sweeping, powerful, tsunami-type redemption that cleanses every facet of our being, leaving in its wake liberty, joy, restoration, peace, and hope.

The truth is this: God's grace and God's desire to redeem and forgive is magnificently greater than any mess we may find ourselves caught up in. We are *all* a mess and God well knows it! That's the very reason he sent his Son to earth.[3]

But here's the thing—at times all I can fixate on are the glaring hypocritical realities of my life regarding even the most elementary teachings of faith and forgiveness. For example:

FORGIVENESS 101

God says, "But I, yes I, am the one who takes care of your sins— that's what I do. I don't keep a list of your sins."[4]

Glaring Reality

God may not, but I sure do! And even though I've asked for forgiveness, there are still things I can neither forget nor forgive myself for doing.

FORGIVENESS 101

"Forgive as quickly and completely as the Master forgave you."[5]

Glaring Reality

Would you like to receive my updated list of *People I Just Can't Forgive* by fax or e-mail?

FORGIVENESS 101

"Surely you know that Christ showed up in order to get rid of sin. There is no sin in him, and sin is not part of his program. No one who lives deeply in Christ makes a practice of sin."[6]

Glaring Reality

I admit a sometimes wavering obedience to the things of God *(despite appearances of outward success and spiritual blessing),* which ultimately leaves me feeling guilty, ashamed, shallow, fake, and useless for the long haul.

Yes, I'm a woman held captive at times by carnal thoughts, selfish motives, and a tendency to rebel rather than obey. But I'm also a woman who is unashamed and unafraid to cry out to God for help. Perhaps I was wired this way in order to grasp the magnitude and depth of divine redemption.

For more than anything, I want to live this present life free and forgiven.

Free and forgiven: falling asleep peacefully at night, accepting the truth that I have been acquitted of everything before.

Free and forgiven: understanding I am desperately loved by One who understands my overwhelming propensity to do what is wrong, even as my heart cries out for what is right.[7]

Free and forgiven: catching a glimpse of the eternal and discerning—perhaps for the first time—what is truly important during my brief decades on planet earth.

In my book *Scandalous Grace* I used words such as *preposterous, outrageous,* and *exorbitant* to introduce the chartreuse-hued color of God's grace. This time around we're going to fill our lexicon of the divine with words such as *revolutionary, relentless,* and *rescue,* as we allow the bold magenta-laden brushstrokes of radical forgiveness to paint a new beginning for our lives.

It's time we dove into the sea of fathomless forgiveness. It's time we experienced—from the soles of our feet to the tips of our highlighted hair strands—the redeeming truth of Jesus Christ, which promises and delivers redemptive mercy and absolute release from that which seems both unforgivable and unforgettable.[8]

Are you ready?

Then here, girlfriend—grab your hanky and take my hand. I'll walk alongside you, listen to your stories, carry the extra bag or two that you brought along, and most importantly, I'll laugh and cry with you *(even sneak you a chocolate HoHo if you like)* every step along the way.

All that remains is to read on. . . .

3

I've Never Told This to Anyone . . .

I shoplifted a pack of AA batteries from Prenger's IGA grocery store when I was 10 years old.

While a student in Mrs. Hayes's elementary class, I allowed Vicky Maddox to take the blame, as well as the corporal swat, for something I did.

In fifth grade I took an "all the good parts are underlined in red ink" paperback of *Love's Avenging Heart* to Mrs. Lockard's classroom. After passing it around to my friends, I got caught red-handed, so to speak, with the bawdy evidence, a few minutes after second recess.

Thinking I was Tony Soprano (or somebody similar) in sixth grade, I leaned on Rodney Brandt and demanded he bring a pan of Rice Krispie treats to school the following day. My La Cosa Nostra ways also included pounding on Mike and Mark Reichert's sack lunches until their potato chips were dust. As a 12-year-old, I made rude and obnoxious prank phone calls and covertly removed a dog-eared copy of *Everything You've Always Wanted to Know about Sex But Were Afraid to Ask* from the local library. I got kicked out of Mr. Kennedy's eighth-grade science class for raising my hand and purposely asking some inane question in the midst of his dissertation regarding the Milky Way. *(In case you're wondering, yes, the sins of the mother have been visited upon her children.)*

And I was almost refused permission to take part in my senior class graduation due to a massive in-school water fight I helped instigate a few days prior.

Mrs. Buffington, Dean of Student Women at Hannibal LaGrange College, failed to appreciate my creative attempts of sneaking in after curfew hours and summoned me once to her office in hopes of dispelling an ugly rumor that I had mooned a fellow dormmate on the third floor of Pulliam Hall. *(Guilty as charged.)* And during a late-night, "let's-get-away-from-studying-for-finals-and-make-an-Oreo-Pepsi-fun-run," I was slapped with a C & I motor vehicle ticket for driving, well, carelessly and imprudently, with seven friends crammed into a souped-up Chevy Camaro.

A positive aside: I didn't receive a ticket for indecent exposure, despite the fact I was wearing only an oversized nightshirt when the 11:30 P.M. imprudent driving took place, and I had failed to see the need for pulling on a pair of shorts or pants before leaving my dorm room.

Moving right along . . .

As a 22-year-old nontenured, first-year elementary teacher, I came "this" close to my principal walking into a teachers' staff meeting and catching me entertaining fellow colleagues with an over-the-top, dead-on impersonation of said administrator.

A few years later I provided anything but comic relief as a

mother of two children who blew up in anger and acted out in a manner that terrified both the children and me.

I spent (literally and figuratively) my early thirties making poor financial choices and creating lies to cover up my actions, and not surprisingly, most of my mid-thirties working to repair the resulting damage to my credit report and relationships.

So there you have it. The lovely Julie Ann Barnhill, in all her glory. *(Or not.)*

I could list my transgressions for pages and pages, and I'm okay with that.

Why? Because we all have our "I've never told this to anyone" secrets. It's just that not all of us are comfortable publishing them for public consumption. But I am. And it doesn't originate out of some perverse need to shock my mother either. No, it's far less Freudian than all that. It stems out of my own inclination of being drawn to the souls who dare to expose their emotional malfunctions, spiritual inconsistencies, and mental ineptness.

Reading or hearing about someone else wrestling with nitty-gritty granules of faith and life makes life *(my life, at least)* more bearable, makes myself more believable. And I need that. Because sometimes I simply cannot believe the stupid things I do. *(And now that you've read some of them, can you believe it either?)*

I'm no saint—not by any stretch of the imagination. But the more I write *(literally keystroke by keystroke)*, the more desperate I become for a revolutionary forgiveness that upends the hidden and surreptitious elements of my life. You see, as hard as it is to believe, given the aforementioned list of sins and infractions,

I tend to be a stealthy sinner—a cloistered screwup. For most of my life I've managed to fly just under the radar of blatant rebellion. Rarely were my sins exposed.

But I knew the truth. And I was scared to death others would find it out too. So, over the years, I devoted a fair amount of time and energy to the task of damage control—through the use of verbal wit and sheer personality I managed to finagle and finesse my way out of trouble and juggle the secrets and sins I was determined to keep safe and hidden. And I did so for quite a number of years.

No one knew I was a liar.

No one knew I was a thief.

No one saw the angry emotions that simmered just beneath the surface.

No one knew after taking my first drink of alcohol I immediately wanted more.

No one knew, for I always (always!) had another lie to tell to cover my tracks. I took small incremental amounts of money that I assumed others wouldn't notice. I held myself in perfect emotional check outwardly and never let anyone know how a scar on my right wrist came to be. *(One evening when I was 14 years old and facing an anger I could neither understand nor control, I bit myself, out of rage and fear, until I bled.)* And I held my liquor well.

However, as I grew older, the secrets *(and sins)* seemed to grow more complex and became more difficult to hide.[1] Ultimately I proved a fundamental truth taught to me from earliest childhood: "You can be sure that your sin will track you down."[2]

And it did—like a relentless bloodhound!

My lying led to hidden debt and financial problems and nearly cost me my marriage. It also revealed the stubborn love of my husband, Rick, as he stayed with me through those bad times. I kept my hands out of others' pocketbooks, but I replaced overt stealing with covetous and greedy thoughts that robbed me of friendships and contentment. The teenage anger that sent me reeling into a fit of self-abuse exploded 12 years later in outbursts of rage and abusive anger toward my two oldest children. And alcohol continued to beckon during periods of loneliness, depression, or when I simply wanted an excuse to do what I knew was wrong. I would succumb *(remember, I am an all-or-nothing female, so when I succumb, I really succumb)*, then feel really guilty *(all-or-nothing guilt too!)*.

✳ ✳ ✳

Whew . . . after I typed those words, I had to stop writing and simply put my head in my hands for a moment. Wouldn't you?

As I reread those confessions now, I wince. I clearly see the trajectory of my life being shaped and formed by secrets and lies. And I can't help but notice that, much like "love and marriage" go together like a horse and carriage, to quote the words of an old song, you can't have one (secrets) without the other (lies).

Perhaps you can relate. Or maybe instead you're thinking, *Yeah, so you told us a few secrets from your life—but none of them can compare to mine.*

You know what? You're probably right. I'm sure if we played a game of "Top This!" some of you could beat me hands down.

But seeing whose sin is worse or who has the most horrifying secret isn't what this is all about. It is, however, about all of us embracing the truth that we are not alone in our secret places. And it is about realizing that no matter what has happened, or what has been said, or what remains hidden beneath layers of deflection and defense mechanisms, God is there, in the very midst.

FORGIVENESS 101

"God knew what he was doing from the very beginning. He decided from the outset to shape the lives of those who love him along the same lines as the life of his Son. The Son stands first in the line of humanity he restored. We see the original and intended shape of our lives there in him."[3]

GLARING REALITY

Our lives are often shaped by lies rather than the truth of Christ and redemption.

The New Testament book of Hebrews encourages us to keep our eyes on Jesus, who both began and finished this race we're in,[4] and to model our thinking about God, others, and ourselves, after the words and actions of him. Jesus is the Road, also the Truth, also the Life,[5] yet we often lose our way along the journey and allow the eyes of heart and mind to settle upon issues and circumstances, sins and failures. And when this happens, we are vulnerable to the Father of Lies.[6]

He's described well as the Designated Accuser,[7] the Prince of the Power of the Air,[8] the Snake,[9] and the Evil One.[10] He is the Thief who comes only to steal and kill and destroy,[11] as well as the Destroyer[12] who has spoken half-truths and falsehoods since time began.[13] He will do whatever he can to keep us from being in a life-changing, love relationship with God. He will tell you lies and try to make you believe God could never forgive you. He will pretend there are things you could do that would make God's love for you end. His name is Satan,[14] and he is the sworn enemy of God and all his creation—this would include you and me.

So much for warm, fuzzy, happy, author thoughts, eh?

I'll grant you those statements may sound a bit, well, funda-mental. But those statements and the Bible portions I quoted from are our only hope for effectively recognizing and rooting out secrets and lies. As women we've covered things up and have made excuses for why we did or didn't do something else (and we'll talk more about these in another chapter, "It's All about Me"). But for the next few paragraphs I want us to con-sider two destructive lies that are at times whispered and at other times shouted to us by our enemy. Lies that infiltrate our thinking, assassinate the character of God, and attempt to nul-lify the glorious realities of both who we are and what we have in Jesus Christ.

LIE #1: YOU'RE THE ONLY ONE WHO'S DONE THE THINGS YOU HAVE.

The Designated Accuser has spoken these words to us from earliest childhood and continues to do so as we live out our life. His subtle accusation is an attempt to steal our joy, kill our spirit, and destroy the bridge (trust in God) that leads to divine forgiveness and freedom.

Few things in life have shamed me or sent me hurtling down a course of condemnation and guilt like the secret of my mothering and anger. While I came across as pretty together outwardly, I knew the verbal and physical boundaries I crossed with my children behind closed doors and drawn curtains. And I wondered if I was the only mother who treated her children so horribly. Or if some other Christian mother was ever overcome by anger and rage.

So one morning I made a confession of sorts to a group of friends—hoping to hear I wasn't alone. But no one said anything—there was dead silence. And as a conversation sprung out of the unnerving silence, I heard the enemy whisper, *I told you no one else has done the things you have. You're despicable and beyond help.*

And I believed him for close to six years. By the end of the seventh year, truth had won out in my life as a mother. God patiently and gently drew me back to the truth of the Bible and began to change my heart in a way that I can only describe as miraculous. My heart and home were filled with forgiveness, laughter, and peace. I vowed if I ever had the opportunity that I would speak openly and honestly about my struggle.

Three years later I had the chance. Before a packed audience I told hundreds of mothers the reality of where I had been and assured them they were not the only ones who had said, done, thought, or considered, whatever they were currently beating themselves up about. I told them we are all a mess and asked them to take the hand of the woman sitting next to them and proclaim this truth, "I am not alone!"

Women lined up to speak with me. One after the other. Some

stood quietly, with their heads bowed. Others fought to regain their composure as the enemy's lie was exposed and defeated. Their conversations, e-mails, and written responses will be forever seared in my memory. I'll never grow tired of hearing another mother say, "Thank you for being honest! The Lord has *truly* shown me I am not the only one who has done the things I've done."

LIE #2: IF ANYONE FINDS OUT WHAT YOU DID, THEY WILL NEVER . . .
   a. love you
   b. want to be around you
   c. understand you
   d. forgive you

We all need somebody to lean on, don't we? We want friends and families that stay with us through thick and thin and love us in spite of our weakness, personality quirks, and mood swings. Songwriters tap into the wellspring of human longing with lyrics that promise you've got a friend and no river, valley, or mountain is going to keep that friend from being there for you. Musicians know, as well as the Liar, that there are few things more frightening than the thought of being rejected and abandoned.

And so Satan builds upon Lie #1. After convincing us we are the only ones who have done such bad things, he further attempts to condemn us and keep us from redemption's power by threatening us with loss: loss of relationships, loss of trust of those who learn of our secrets, and the loss of no longer being able to hide behind our mask of deceit.

The truth is, some of those you consider friends may leave you once they find out certain truths. It's happened to me—from both sides. Friends have dropped me once they learned about the depth of some of my messes. And I once dropped a friend cold turkey after learning some uncomfortable details. The truth is, "friends come and friends go, but a true friend sticks by you like family."[15] I wasn't much of a family to my friend, but Jesus always is. Time and time again he promises us he will never leave us. Time and time again he welcomes us when we have turned from him and gone our own way. Despite the Liar, who tries to convince us otherwise, Jesus never gives up on us— even if we give up on him. "For there's no way he can be false to himself."[16]

So there you have it. Why have I confessed? Why have I admitted that I don't have it all together? Well, I've done it for *you.*

I've lived enough years and experienced enough failure to know that our secrets and our sins will never be taken care of in and through our own power or any "I can do it" thinking.

God knows we've tried . . . and failed miserably. He knows our messes of magnificent proportions run deep and penetrate the very core of who we are as women and as believers. And he knows we long to be free—to know what it's like to be released from the weight, whether real or perceived, of sins alluded to a few paragraphs ago.

You see, I need someone to rescue my mind, my heart, my will. I long for my present life to be redeemed—I want to experience, to embrace, to believe in a radical redemption that sweeps across the canvas of my soul—leaving its indelible, magenta-hued brushstroke. *(Okay, so I need some really bright colors to get my attention! What about you?)*

I want radical redemption that promises and delivers freedom—not just for the moment, or the month *(although I'd take that too)*—but forever. My soul cries out for radical redemption that upends my religious, neat, tidy, and often ineffective world; a rescue that goes to whatever length, whatever width, whatever height, and whatever depth, to deliver me from secrets and shame.[17]

Maybe you feel that redemption is far from your reach—or even your ability to comprehend. But there still burns within you a desire for things noble, good, and true.[18]

If you're tired of pretending you have it all together, now's the time to take action. For far too long, women—Christian women in particular—have believed they are the only ones dealing with secret sins, shameful issues, agonizing regrets, and more than a skeleton or two hanging in their closet. And because women have kept these secrets in their closets, those secrets are destroying their lives.

But if we dare to open up—to God, ourselves, and others—we can experience an exhilarating freedom and peace. We can say yes to truth and no to the power of secrets and lies, knowing that not even the worst sins listed in Scripture can drive a wedge between us and Christ's love.[19] Just listen to what these women have told me:

✳ I can't believe I'm writing you this letter. Last night you prayed for the women attending the conference and asked God to reveal any and all lies or secrets and to then direct us to someone we could trust and share them with. Well, I pick you, Julie. I've never told anyone this before, but I simply can't live with the secret, the shame, and the guilt one more day. Here goes: I had a sexual relationship with a woman during my early twenties, and I can never forgive myself. I know you'll read this tonight and when I listen to you tomorrow, it's going to seem better, having finally told someone.

✳ Talk about personal! As you told us your secrets, I began to cry. And then sob. And eventually bawl. You may have noticed my shoulders heaving in the back row! My secret is . . . I had an abortion when I was 18 years old. No one knows about it. Not the father of the child. Not my parents. Not even my best friend. For 14 years, I have placed a small black mark on July 12th of my desk calendar and have grieved for the child no one knew about and the young woman who bore the guilt alone. But no more, Julie! Now I know I am not alone, and for the first time in my life, I truly believe God is bigger than my secret—and willing to forgive. *(Which I have asked him to do time and time again, but for some reason, I truly believe it today!)*

✳ I confessed my secret to my girlfriends last night. I have shaken and thrown my three-year-old daughter. I also told them about being physically abused as a child. It feels like a boulder has been lifted off my heart.

✳ I have what I consider an "eternal" secret that I can't ever imagine being forgiven. When I was in college, God asked me to talk to a young man I had been extremely close to in high school. Talk to as in "tell him about Jesus and how much he loves him." Well, I didn't do it. All I could think about was how gorgeous he was and how he'd probably look at me and ask, "And you are??" God said go, and I said no. Just a few months later I found out he had died of a drug overdose. And all I can think about is how lonely and rejected he must have felt and how much I miss him and how I wish I could go back for just two minutes and tell him I love him and Jesus loves him too . . . it feels good to be writing this. Maybe there is forgiveness to be found after all.

The truth is, you're not the only woman with a secret life (or harboring secrets forced upon you by others' sins). Sharing them with someone you trust is a key step toward radical forgiveness.[20] Secrets hold their power only when they are hidden. Once placed in the light of God's love and revealed, they lose their power. Why not make today the day you clean those secrets out of your hidden closet? The day you refuse to give them power over your life anymore?

And you might be surprised who else is struggling with the same things.

Déjà Vu . . . All Over Again

4

𝒥 have always wanted to be original.

It was evident through the wild tales I told my Dad and Bill Greene while sitting around the community round table at Moser's Coffee Shop. It was also evident in my choice of purple-hued spiked hair in 1983 and the sassy pair of stiletto-heeled chartreuse boots I recently purchased.

I'm a woman who hides her newest issues of *In Style* and *Allure* in order to be the first to read their original contents. *(I know it sounds a little twisted but I once heard comedian Jerry Seinfeld confess to the same psychosis involving newspapers. Ah, now I feel better.)*

I revel in discovering original authors and books and preface every true girlfriend conversation with, "Oh! You have got to read . . ."

I bristle at the thought of actually reading an *Oprah, Kelly,* or *Today Show* book pick. After all, if one million other women are reading it, how original can my discovering it be? *(Disclaimer: I did allow my first book,* She's Gonna Blow, *to be plugged on the Oprah show. I may be twisted, but I'm not stupid.)*

Yes, indeed, there's a certain rush, a certain intrinsic thrill when you believe you have created, accomplished, or thought in some manner that can be attributed to your distinct, original self.

This would be the creative mind-set I had when approaching the editors at Tyndale House Publishers about creating an online women's survey discussing the subject of redemption and forgiveness. I wanted to find out what women were really thinking about these broad and as hard-to-nail-down-as-Jell-O concepts. I wanted to go where no author had gone before, creating a one-of-a-kind original survey that allowed participants the opportunity to get past canned yes or no answers and to share instead the vast number of areas in their lives in which forgiveness was hard to accept or give. I was convinced Dr. Phil himself had yet to unearth said information.

Watch out! Julie had a dog to hunt!

Within a matter of days cyber genius Victor Kore created and forwarded said e-friendly survey to the in-boxes of 500 women. I waited anxiously to read their responses.

Four weeks later, after reading through the compiled pages of comments, I thought better of hunting that dog I mentioned. Despite my ballyhooed beliefs of "vast this" and "untapped that," the comments, statements, and heartbreakingly honest confessions of participants responding placed their struggles with forgiveness in one of three categories.

Three.

Not 12, 20, or 100.

Three.

I couldn't believe it. Figuring the computer had to be wrong,

I grabbed a pen and paper and created a tally sheet of my own. Line by line I read through the information and placed each response under an appropriate category—over and over until I found myself looking at hundreds of tally marks neatly lined beneath three headings:

✳ Sexual choices and their consequences
✳ Body and weight matters
✳ Relationship with God

Well, I'll be. I guess I should have paid more attention to a wise man named Solomon who rather cryptically cautioned, "Does someone call out, 'Hey, this is new'? Don't get excited—it's the same old story."[1]

Same old story, indeed.

An "aha!" mental synapse triggered a memory, and I quickly logged into Word research documents I had saved for the writing of *Scandalous Grace.* Bringing up a file titled *Let It Go,* I began to skim through its contents. And there I found it. Survey comments from hundreds of other women who, having spent a weekend considering God's scandalous grace and letting go of specific pain and struggle, had responded to the following question, "What is your greatest fear and/or spiritual disappointment as a woman?"

I had listed a few examples in *Scandalous Grace* on pages 11 and 12 and decided, this day, to review and tally the entire lot according to their appropriate category. I had a good idea what the outcome was going to be this time. Sure enough, the majority of fears and disappointments fell under the similar headings of my original survey: sexual choices and their consequences, body image, and one's relationship with God.

It seems I'd tapped into something original after all, but I wasn't the first person to figure it out. For that I need to quote cryptic Solomon again: "What was will be again, what happened will happen again. There's nothing new on this earth. Year after year it's the same old thing."[2] I'm thinking Solomon could have used a Prozac or two; nevertheless, he nailed it on the head. There really *isn't* anything new to the human condition.

✳ Good times, bad times; war and peace
✳ Sunshine, floods; feasts and famines
✳ Joy, depression; laughter and wailing
✳ Kindness, greed; hatred and murder
✳ Marriage, divorce; births and funerals
✳ Lust, envy; contentment and love

Humankind has been there, done that. And it appears the truth rings true for womankind as well . . .

✳ Cellulite, stretch marks; bickerings and heartaches
✳ Pregnancies, infertility; career advancement and lay-offs
✳ Washboard abdomens, tummy-tucks; MENSA applications and disabilities
✳ Promises kept, dreams realized; foreclosures and menopause
✳ Fathers who stayed, mothers who held us; joint custody and adoption
✳ Faithfulness, intimacy; promiscuity and regret

And the fact that all of us struggle, to a greater or lesser extent, with forgiveness.

✳   ✳   ✳

Forgiveness. Gulp. It's a big word, fraught with connotations we're somehow never ready for. My guess is that you probably have at least one book on a dusty shelf *(life is too short for dusting, right, girls?)* that addresses the subject, and you may have tuned into a daytime talk show and overheard Dr. Expert explaining what forgiveness is and how it works. Any relationship counselor worth their salt also uses the word, as do mothers or teachers attempting to referee two or more sparring siblings or classmates. Let's face it: The word and concept are parried about quite a bit.

But what does forgiveness *really* mean?

From our earliest playground experiences we are instructed in matters of forgiveness.

"Okay, say you're sorry," one mother demands of her child who has just whacked a playmate on the head or said something mean.

"Sorry," the child whispers just beneath her breath.

"Now tell her you forgive her," the other mother demands of her child.

"I forgive you," that child parrots—though not believing a word of what she's saying and still feeling the sting of the whack on the head or the unkind words.

And time passes. The playground is dug up and replaced with a parking lot, but the dynamics of life remain the same. We fuss

and fight with family and friends, accumulate a host of memories—some good, some bad—and find ourselves mulling over
perceived slights and flat-out wrongs. And while technically we
may go through the motions and say the "right" words and do
our "good Christian duty," we still walk away, much like that
younger girl, still carrying the weight of a grudge, feeling the
sting of the pain, and not believing a word she has just said.
And we wonder, *What's wrong with me?*

But is it supposed to be as easy as all that? Can repeating
just a few words—the magical phrase "I forgive you"—transform
any hurdles you face in the area of forgiveness? Is there something wrong with you? Are you the only woman who has found
the concept of forgiveness difficult, if not impossible, to live out
in your day-to-day life?

Let me assure you, you are not! Don't forget—more than
500 REAL women* took part in a survey and boldly shared their
stories and heartaches with me.

Here are a few of their responses:

✳ I have had a hard time forgiving my dad for the way he
   yelled at me and how emotionally distant he was from
   me as a child. I feel like we have a good relationship now,
   but I know I've put up walls so he won't get too close—
   I don't want to let him in to certain places of my heart.

✳ I thought I was "all over" the stuff about my parents'
   divorce. Then I had my children, and it seems like a whole
   new can of worms has opened up.

* Since individuals responded anonymously to the survey, all proper names, as
well as certain details referring to e-mail, telephone, or handwritten responses,
have been changed to protect the identity of the writers.

✳ I struggle to forgive my in-laws for the way they treated my husband as a child.

✳ I slept around with a lot of men before I was married. Anytime I see one of them in my hometown, I feel dirty and ashamed—and wonder if my husband has any idea how bad I am.

✳ I was very cruel to my younger sister. No matter how many times she tells me she has forgiven me . . . well, I don't believe it. I wouldn't forgive me if I were her!

✳ I lied to my husband about our finances. BIG lies. I can't imagine why he forgave me, but he did. If he had done the same thing, I would have been seething—and I wouldn't have let it go.

✳ I'm 34 years old and just learned I am the product of a rape. Why would my mom keep this from me for so long? And why did God allow it to happen?

✳ One memory haunts me to this day: I totally lost it after a day of my smart-aleck daughter's ways. I screamed at her so loud the windows were probably shaking, and I threw her against the wall and onto her bed. She was 12 years old at the time (18 now), and I still can't shake it from my mind.

✳ My husband left me after 29 years of marriage. He told me he never loved me. Now I spend my days either plotting his demise or attempting to cover up the pain of his leaving.

Do any of these stories sound familiar? Do you have a story of your own to add—an area of deep pain?

Indeed we are all in this together, and there is nothing new under the sun. Even after accepting God's preposterous grace (for more on that, refer to *Scandalous Grace*) for ourselves, does that mean we can snap our fingers and everything in life has a quick fix? Does it mean the act of forgiving is easy? Especially if you call yourself a Christian and know that's what you're supposed to do?

Consider the situation I'm grappling with right now. I learned last night that there is a convicted sex offender (victim under 18) living two blocks from our home. Immediately my gut knotted. I had my two older children look at his photo online (Illinois Registry of Sexual Offenders) and then talked to my husband about how we should inform other families in the town about this man.

I called the Sheriff's Department and Illinois State Police to find out what my rights were as a concerned parent. *(Make that outraged, fearful, repulsed, and worried parent.)* Moments after hanging up the phone, my 14-year-old son asked me, "Mom, what if that guy has changed? Aren't we supposed to forgive him? And isn't it mean for you to be talking to people about him?"

Hmm. My jaw dropped open a degree or two. My immediate response was to launch into a passionate and well-sanitized lecture about sexual offenders and what they do and how they prey on children. I told my son in vociferous terms that I had researched such crime and the statistics, and such research revealed that it is difficult for sexual offenders to change their behavior patterns. As I spoke, images of other children on our block, in our neighborhood, living in our community, came to mind. How I would hate it if one of them—much less one of my own children—were hurt by this man!

And so, as a result of this situation, I'm wrestling even more with the beliefs I say I have and the ugly reality of one man's sin. Today I know I answered none of my son's questions, but I raised a few more of my own:

✳ Does a convicted child sexual offender technically qualify for the "love your neighbor" status? Or does Jesus have an "excluded category" somewhere?

✳ How do I know that this man won't hurt my children or someone else's? Are there any fool-safe guarantees?

✳ And if this man has the potential to hurt children again, wouldn't it be crazy for me to assume the best (that he has changed) and foolishly disregard his past? How "on my guard" should I be, and what does that mean practically?

✳ Does forgiveness mean I agree to let all consequences go? (Certainly not. The law says this man will always have to be listed with the IRSO. No matter where he moves, his neighbors will need to be notified regarding his past actions.)

✳ Does it mean I should allow this man to be in my home for any reason—or to be around my children?

✳ Does forgiveness mean total trust?

✳ ✳ ✳

As I talked with women across the nation and read their revelations via e-mail and letter, something clicked. I realized that our three biggest areas of struggle and remorse—sexual choices and their consequences, body image, and one's relationship with God—are directly linked with the three areas in which we need to experience radical forgiveness:

FORGIVING OTHERS FOR THE AWFUL THINGS THEY DO.
Has someone betrayed you or caused you grief? Perhaps you find yourself hating someone for what he or she has done to you. Maybe you can relate to Diane, who writes,

𝕴 have tried over and over to forgive my mother. When I was a young girl, I told her the truth about what my dad had done to me *(sexual abuse),* and she called me a liar. She told me he would never do those things to me, and she didn't understand why I would make up such horrible lies. It's been over 25 years, and still she has never admitted the truth, nor have I *ever* forgiven her.

Or to Kari, who admitted,

𝕴 absolutely hate my father-in-law. He has gone out of the way to make my husband's life miserable—and mine too. The last time we were at their house, he told me, "I don't know why Kevin ever married you. You're not what we wanted." I had to run out of the house before I started sobbing . . . and I never want to go back. I love my husband, but he insists that as Christians, we need to stay involved with his family, even when it's hurtful. I'm just not sure how much more I can take.

FORGIVING GOD FOR WHAT HE HAS DONE— OR HASN'T DONE—IN YOUR LIFE.

This area brings up a host of questions in and of itself. Perhaps you've asked, "If God is all-powerful, then why didn't he stop what happened from happening?" Or, "What did I do to deserve what I'm getting? Doesn't God like me?"

Maybe you feel like Andrea, who revealed,

*E*verywhere I look, I see couples. And then there's me, still single and not loving it. Every time I read Romans 8:28, "All things work for good," I get angry. Being single for me isn't good. I long to have a partner. What's wrong with God anyway? He's the one who came up with Adam not wanting to be alone, so he created Eve. Why doesn't God grant me my desire for a husband? I pray and pray . . . I live the best Christian life I can. But nothing happens. The honest truth? God has let me down, and I'm finding it hard to believe in him anymore.

Or Meagan, who said,

*T*hree years ago our home burned to the ground while we were on vacation. I lost everything that was important to me. Family heirlooms, photos of my two kids as babies, and the one thing I had left from my mother, who died when I was young—her piano. I'm still grieving. I can't believe God would allow that to happen. All of those are things, yes, but I'll never get them back. God had to know how much they meant to me. How could he allow that to happen? And during the one "big" vacation that our family had taken in years? It seems like such a dirty trick . . . whatever happened to the saying, "God has our best in mind?"

FORGIVING YOURSELF.

Ouch. This is probably the diciest one. Who of us wants to admit the yuck in our life to ourselves, much less anyone else? Especially if that person is going to hold us accountable to do something about the yuck? *(Why is it that we can unburden ourselves to strangers in the seat next to us on the airplane, but we can't talk with the ones we love about what's bothering us?)*

Carol, who just turned 39, wrote,

A month ago I miscarried my second baby, and I know it's all my fault. If I hadn't messed around in my early twenties, if I'd married earlier, I wouldn't be almost 40, with no child. And that's all I've ever wanted—to be a mom. Now the clock's ticking, and I feel it every day. . . . How can I ever forgive myself?

And then there's Dana, who's 26, but still living through the aftermath of a date rape when she was 19.

I wish I could go back and do it all over. Wish I would have said no to dating that guy. But he seemed so nice—who would have known? Sure, I've talked to a counselor, and I "know" it wasn't my fault. It had nothing to do with me, but everything to do with the fact the guy was violent . . . and, well, *sick.* But I can't help it. I wake up a lot at night feeling dirty, wondering, *If I hadn't worn that short skirt, would he still have raped me?* I can never forgive myself for being so stupid.

(Note: Even if a difficult thing is perpetrated upon us, we women often still feel at fault and guilty.)

Living a redeemed life—a radically forgiven life—doesn't mean you will have no temptations. Or that you won't have days where you feel like the ugly duckling, like worthless garbage, like a mess of magnificent proportions *(just ask me— I ought to know!).* And there will be days when you're just plain . . . well, ticked off and mad. As wise Solomon knew, those oh-so-human feelings will always be with us.

But living with a view of redemption—of what forgiveness really means—can free us to live life "in the meanwhile." To accept ourselves and our human condition as God accepts us. To truly love ourselves, God, and others—even when we don't feel lovely or deserving.

5

It's All about Me

am I the only woman who's gazed into the mirror and been
less than pleased with the reflection looking back?

And please note: It isn't the result of wrinkles, forgetting to
remove my makeup from the night before, or the increasingly
noticeable white hairs springing defiantly from my head. Nah
. . . a 12-week run of Retin-A créme, a dollop of Cetaphil
cleanser, and a dazzling tricolor foil coiffeur at Studio 117 set-
tles those issues well enough. No, this nagging sense of disappointment deep within me has nothing to do with my physical
hang-ups and everything to do with the spiritual ones.

Time and time again, I've been befuddled, perplexed, and
stymied by my inability to handle *(um, perhaps control is a better
word)* my actions and choices in given situations. And I wince
at my less-than-stellar track record of remaining on the straight
and narrow. Honestly. "What I don't understand about myself
is that I decide one way, but then I act another, doing things
I absolutely despise."[1]

Sigh. And many of the women surveyed admit to the same
thing.

✳ Every morning I wake up and vow, *Today I'm going to control my anger*. And I mean it, I really mean it. But then I can't find the keys to my car or my assistant fails to tell me of an important deadline change in the project I'm overseeing. Then faster than you can imagine, I'm ranting and raving and acting like a complete moron. Time and time again.

✳ I eat all the time. I wake up thinking about food and spend the majority of my day planning what I'm going to eat. Late at night, when my family is fast asleep, I look at myself in the mirror and promise yet again to stop. But it never seems to last.

✳ There is a man I can't stop thinking about. And he's not my husband. Every day I tell myself this is ridiculous and wrong. I've even told my sister about him and asked her to help me get over him. But you know what I do instead? I lie to my sister and find ways to run into him unexpectedly. No one has to tell me this is wrong. No one has to make me feel bad (I feel miserable!). Yet I can't seem to do the right thing.

It seems pretty clear to me. We all need some help in at least one area of our life. *(That's kind of nice to know, huh? That neither you nor I are alone in our "help me" prayers?)* And consider this: We'll go a lot further and faster when we admit that we need help, rather than stuffing that need into a dark corner and pretending it's not there. What human being hasn't gotten sucked into at least one of the Me, Me, Me! Realities? Take, for instance:

ME, ME, ME! REALITY #1

"Something has gone wrong deep within me and gets the better of me every time."[2]

Isn't that the truth? I'm so thankful the saintly apostle Paul was both willing and gutsy enough to admit his struggles. It gives the rest of us hope! The first time I read Romans 7:19-21, I sighed with relief. If any two verses summed up my situation, it was indeed those two, for day by day my sin seems to get the better of me. No matter how much I read the Bible, attend church, and participate in many other "Christian" activities, I'm still hit in the head with my need: "But I need something *more!* For if I know the law but still can't keep it, and if the power of sin within me keeps sabotaging my best intentions, I obviously need help! . . ."[3]

That I—that we—"obviously need help" is an understatement, don't you think? But don't despair—help IS on the way.

Thus far in *Radical Forgiveness,* we've talked about our magnificent mess, confessed a few secrets, and considered the areas we struggle with as a forgiving or a forgiven woman. But those three things alone fail to explain why we do what we do and why, so often, we choose to do the wrong thing. To find the answer to those questions, we're going to have to dig a bit deeper and expose ourselves to some pretty pointed truths.

So many women (myself included) have a difficult time sensing the redemptive, forgiven life. We go through the motions of religious service, church attendance, positive talk, and sometimes embrace iffy teachings on spiritualism in hopes of quelling the fear, the shame, the disappointment, and the embarrassment that we aren't really who we claim to be in the inner places of life.

And it's certainly not from lack of trying. Bible studies, prayer journals, numerous church activities, and nightstands loaded down with the latest best sellers, promising dynamic, purposeful living, all testify to our dogged attempts to "do better."

So why—after studying 12 books of the Old Testament, or praying 15 more minutes than we did yesterday, or attending the latest women's retreat, or upon closing the back cover of our "Must Read" book—do we still feel so lousy? And can somebody please tell me why we never seem to get any better at "doing better"?

Time and again I've vowed to stop doing something—and ended up doing it. Time and again I've closed the door to one temptation or sin—just to take on a different one completely. It's enough to make a girl feel like a big Christian jellyfish *(no spine, no heart, and no brain)* who has just flopped on a sandy tropical beach and is in the process of drying up.

Is there any hope for us? Yes! But it all has to start with understanding how we got to where we are. There is no limit to the "dark" places, the "big and ugly" sins that could be exposed within each of us. But that is exactly why we need God's scandalous grace to cover and ferret out those dark places, and that is exactly why we need to experience the washing of his radical forgiveness.

ME, ME, ME! REALITY #2

"Basically, all of us, whether insiders or outsiders, start out in identical conditions, which is to say that we all start out as sinners. Scripture leaves no doubt about it."[4]

Rocker Annie Lennox once sang "I was born an original sinner." A man named David once observed, "I've been out of step with you for a long time, in the wrong since before I was born."[5] This truth is also expressed in another Bible translation: "Behold I was brought forth in iniquity, and in sin my mother conceived me."[6]

Well! I'll bet you haven't seen *that* printed on many baby announcements. Such a statement would ruin the sweet picture of innocence in that new life we love to goo-goo over and cuddle.

Nevertheless, Annie and David are both right. All of our hearts, all of our minds, and all of our souls, have been stained by sin. What do I mean when I use the word *sin*? Is sin as simple and lightweight as an oops-a-daisy or a mistake? No, sin is far different. It's the *deliberate* choosing to go against God's way and follow our own way. And we humans (and I include myself in this) are very good at sinning. We've been doing it for a long time. It all started way back with Adam and Eve—it's all their fault *(yes, I know—I'm passing the buck, but they deserve it, don't you think?).*

I like the way writer Eugene Peterson phrases it in *The Message*: "You know the story of how Adam landed us in the dilemma we're in—first sin, then death, and no one exempt from either sin or death. That sin disturbed relations with God in everything and everyone."[7]

It is the story of Eve, deceived by the one referred to as the Serpent. And it's the story of Adam, who willfully chose to disobey the loving commands of God. *(You can read all the details in chapters 1–3 of the Old Testament book of Genesis.)* It is the story of Us—the women of today who bear the mark of humanity and all its consequences.

This is why our natural inclination is to do the wrong over the right.

This is why we can't make ourselves be good.

This is why we rebel against absolutes—especially divine absolutes.

This is why we need—no, we crave—radical forgiveness in divine form.

To put it simply, without God's help, we start out sinful and we end sinful.

A few years ago, I traveled to New Orleans for a Christian convention. I had never visited the city of jazz and Bourbon Street, and made it my priority to put on a comfortable pair of walking shoes and check out all the narrow streets and rich historical sites that I could. One afternoon, after doing just that, I boarded an air-conditioned shuttle bus and overheard the conversation between two other convention attendees. *(The 4x4 name badges affixed to their jackets gave them away.)* I can't remember the exact details, but they basically lamented the fact that the convention was being held in such a wicked place and proceeded to list off four or five specific sins they had observed someone *(not me, I hope!)* committing while there. The attendees were quick to note these "sinful" people were probably not Christians. Soon enough the two attendees exited the bus and returned to the safe Christian confines of the convention floor.

But I couldn't get that conversation out of my head. I headed off to dinner, and in the middle of crab legs and filet, it hit me. Here were two women, two Christian women, I presumed, who found the idea of men and women committing sin to be, well, shocking. So much so that they referred to the entire area of

New Orleans as Sin City and wanted to disassociate themselves from it as quickly as possible. And yet they seemed to have no idea how many folks had overheard their discussion—and had been turned off by their gossipy form of Christianity.

That's what really bothered me. But then I realized it was kind of like calling the kettle black. After all, I was listening in on their conversation and judging them without too much thought.

And I was left thinking, *Isn't this exactly what sinners do?*

All too often, when left to our devices, we choose to sin. There is a root of sinful self-interest in us[8] that is at odds with what God desires. And as a result of our leaning into the sinful, self-motivated ways of living, we get "repetitive, loveless, cheap sex; a stinking accumulation of mental and emotional garbage; frenzied and joyless grabs for happiness; trinket gods; magic-show religion; paranoid loneliness; cutthroat competition; all-consuming-yet-never-satisfied wants; a brutal temper; an impotence to love or be loved; divided homes and divided lives; small-minded and lopsided pursuits; the vicious habit of depersonalizing everyone into a rival; uncontrolled and uncontrollable addictions; ugly parodies of community. I could go on"[9]. . . but is there any need? Clearly, we are women in need of rescue—extreme soul rescue!

On one hand it IS all about me—about us. It's about us in that we realize how human we are and that we've made good, as well as bad, choices as a result of our humanness and experience.

But on the other hand it's NOT all about me—or you. We all started with the same "heart condition" *(once again thank you,*

Adam and Eve), and we all need the same cure (one that we'll discuss more thoroughly in the chapter to come).

ME, ME, ME! REALITY #3

"It happens so regularly that it's predictable. The moment I decide to do good, sin is there to trip me up."[10] "I've tried everything and nothing helps. I'm at the end of my rope."[11]

Sarah, a petite beauty who really looks like she has it all together, admitted she felt that way. It was a big risk for her to reveal what was going on in her life, but with tears rolling down her cheeks, she finally did:

If I could take back the last five years of my life, I would. But I know I can't. And because of me and the choices I made, my kids are now suffering. I just found out last night that my daughter, who just turned 15, is pregnant. After her daddy left because of my affair with a coworker, she's been "looking for love in all the wrong places." As much as I love her, I know I've failed her. I'm the one who has done wrong, and she's the one who is paying for it. Every morning I hate getting up, knowing I have to live with myself one more day.

Come on, girlfriend, are you there? At the end of your rope? Do you understand, deep in your soul, what despair is? If so, it's time to take a risk. You have nothing to lose and everything to gain. Keep reading!

ME, ME, ME! REALITY #4

Here's a hard truth: We will never be sinless and perfect, but we have to *want* change.

Gulp. Now that's hitting the nail on the head.

- ✳ Lying
- ✳ Losing my temper and spouting off verbally
- ✳ Spending money I don't have for things I don't need
- ✳ Bucking authority
- ✳ Holding grudges
- ✳ Judging myself, and other women, by outward appearances as well as overheard conversations

Yup, that's a good list of my sins *(some of yours too?)* and I'm no longer shocked when they rear their fat, ugly heads.

Unfortunately, it's clear that all of us get caught in the cycle of sin and messing up. But what's not so clear is how badly we really want to stop.

Mmm. Consider these words women penned in the write-in portion of the survey:

- ✳ I'm a gossip, a bad gossip. And as soon as I open my mouth or listen with my Dumbo-sized gossip ears, I start to feel bad. But I keep talking and listening and then repeat everything to my mother or sisters. Yes, I'm a Christian, but I sure don't act much like one. And yes, I've tried to quit but it's really hard. I just can't seem to stop myself.

- ✳ I rarely read the Bible. I know I should. I buy devotional books and say I'm going to go through them, but let's be honest: I'd rather sit down with a historical romance when it comes right down to it.

- ✳ No one—and I mean NO ONE—would believe I'm an alcoholic. I'm not even sure my husband does. I started drinking when I was 19 and have barely gone a day without at least one drink. I can't tell you how ashamed I am of this fact. Nor can I tell you how afraid I am to let anyone know.

✳ If worry is a sin, then I'm the biggest sinner on the face of the earth. I worry about my health (will I get cancer like my mom did?). I worry about my adult daughter (will she get cancer and does she go for yearly exams like I told her to?). I worry if I'll have enough money to live on when I retire in three years. I worry about terrorist activity in the metropolitan area where I live. I know I'm supposed to trust God, but how do I know he's really going to take care of those things anyway? Where's the guarantee?

This would be where the rubber meets the me, me, me road.

On one hand, we need to acknowledge our human propensity to sin. Yes, we are sinners. We are born sinners, and we will always be sinners. None of us is perfect stacked up next to a sinless, perfect God.

But does that mean we have no control over our actions—since we're destined to sin and will always sin, should we even try to do otherwise?

Certainly not. God wants—and expects—us to take responsibility for the part we willfully play in our sinful behavior and choices. Read through the above comments from the surveyed women one more time. You'll notice each of the ladies who spoke of her sin also gave a reason *(or weak excuse)* for holding on to it.

The first lady was basically saying, "Well, it's just too hard, so I'm not going to try."

The second one was saying, "I'm plain lazy, and like to do what's easiest and least challenging."

The third lady was saying, "If I reveal my secret, no one will like me anymore. They'll think I'm a horrible person."

The fourth woman wanted to bargain with God. "God, if you do things my way, then I won't worry anymore."

Is it possible, if we were to be completely honest, that more than a few of us like our rut more than the idea of the work of getting out of it?

Hey! This is TrimSpa girl talking to you! I know what it's like to want an instant fix—and with as little pain and effort as possible, thank you very much. I want to feel better—have less guilt, know my Bible better, lose weight—but I also still want to have a good time *(translation: do what I want)*.

And why is that, do you suppose? Is it because we don't really want to let go of the excuses, the rationalizations, the hurt, to truly embrace the big, theological, scary concepts of redemption and forgiveness—and what they truly mean in our life—on a daily basis? Is it possible that we are more than a little afraid that somehow what we're going to get (as a result of obeying God and allowing God to rescue our life and send us in a different direction—the direction he wants us to go instead of our own) won't necessarily be better—and might quite possibly be a lot less fun?

I believe those are perfectly legitimate questions to ask. And even better ones to answer. Because, quite often, all we do is offer up excuses for our sin, rather than embrace the sin and ask for God's help to stop it.

WHAT WE SAY

"It's not my fault."

WHAT WE MEAN

I'm not willing to accept responsibility for this, so I'm going to pass the buck.

WHAT WE SAY

"It's not as bad as all that."

WHAT WE MEAN

Well, at least I'm not as bad as . . .

WHAT WE SAY

"She's a lot worse than I am."

WHAT WE MEAN

I don't believe I'm all that bad.

WHAT WE SAY

"He doesn't deserve to be treated well."

WHAT WE MEAN

He's a scum. I refuse to forgive him for what he did.

It's funny. Despite our generation's thirst for tabloid television and "bare it all" journalism, we still don't want to admit our own shortcomings and sins. Think about it. When was the last time you heard someone admit: "I knew that was wrong, but I wanted to do it, so I did it anyway"? And when's the last time you didn't hear someone rationalize, "I do this because I felt abandoned as a child, my mother didn't love me enough, and I have low self-esteem"?

You see, there are things that happened to us that truly are *not* our fault (e.g., abuse as a child. We'll discuss these issues in the chapter "Forgive and Forget? . . . and Other Myths"). But that doesn't change the fact that we sometimes use the past, or our present conditions, as an excuse for present bad choices and behavior.

Once again, in *Radical Forgiveness,* I find myself writing out of my own journey of faith and life. Not as an expert, heaven forbid.

You see, the more time I spend in this life, the more I realize that I'm a mess who longs for God to take the broken, sinful pieces of her life and self and create a work of restoration, renewal, and hope. I need to probe the limitless power of divine forgiveness. To contemplate and wrap my mind around God's willingness (and rightful authority) to sanitize and wipe clean the entire slate of my life's history.

I believe the majority of us do want to do better. We long to do better. And the nagging question of where we will go for help and whom we can depend on is answered again by Paul, who doesn't end his teachings in Romans with us swimming in a pit of despair.

Encouraging all me, me, me sinners and saints, he declares, "The answer, thank God, is that Jesus Christ can and does. He acted to set things right in this life of contradictions where I want to serve God with all my heart and mind, but am pulled by the influence of sin to do something totally different."[12]

And that, my friends, is the exact purpose of redemption.

To remove the stain of sin, disobedience, foolishness, shame, regret, and self-sufficient pride, and present us clean—before God and the reflection gazing back at us each morning.

Because really, isn't that woman in the mirror the hardest person to convince?

6

Trading Spaces

What do you get when you put together two couples, two designers, one carpenter, and a thousand-dollar budget, to be spent in two days decorating each other's homes?

* Spray-painted furniture
* Circus-tent ceilings
* Hay-covered walls
* Weepy homeowners
* And transformed rooms!

You can always count on a lot of laughter, as well as seeing some pretty ticked-off folks on the popular decorating program, *Trading Spaces. (Yikes! Do you remember decorator Doug and the reaction of the couple whose fireplace he covered with wainscoting? Scary, I tell you. Plumb scary.)* Suffice it to say not every trade works out, and some of the designers' décor choices are, well, downright sinful to look at.

But in real life and in God's economy, sin is no laughing matter. Sin—any sin—is serious because it separates us from

God, who is holy, perfect, and sinless. You may recall our discussion about Adam and Eve in the previous chapter. "One man's sin put crowds of people *(uh, make that all of humanity past, present, and future)* at the dead-end abyss of separation from God."[1] Now that's scary!

But even though our sins are serious, God hasn't, in disgust, left us in the dust. He has provided a way of radical forgiveness. And this way—the one Way—is God's Son, Jesus Christ. Jesus "traded spaces" with you, and his is the only trade that comes with a "satisfaction guarantee." [2] The apostle Paul counsels us once again to consider, "Just think what God's gift poured through one man, Jesus Christ, will do! There's no comparison between that death-dealing sin *[of Adam]* and this generous, life-giving gift."[3]

Because of all your sin, you deserved to die on that cross. But Jesus "traded spaces" with you—and you definitely got the better end of the deal. He took your place on the cross—a place of pain and agony not only physically but also emotionally. When he chose to do his Father's will, to take on all of humankind's sin, Jesus also agreed that, for a time, he would be separated from God.

The weight of your sins, my sins, all humankind's sins—must have been enormous. But because of Jesus' sacrifice, God's forgiveness is infinite. And, you can know, just as Christian musician Steve Camp's song declares, "He Is All You Need."

TRADING SPACES TRUTH #1
"Here it is in a nutshell: Just as one person did it wrong and got us in all this trouble with sin and death, another person did it right and got us out of it."[4]

Jesus and the Cross—it's the most significant turning point of anyone's life. It's the point at which we will all stand some-day and make our choice. We will say yes, we will say no, or we will just stand there, mute. But it's important to know that not choosing doesn't get us off the hook—it doesn't make us immune from the consequences, either. Not choosing IS making a choice—to do nothing.

You may feel totally unworthy and *know* you need to accept Jesus' sacrifice for you. Or you may think, *Hey, I'm not so bad, I know this guy who* . . . But in the hierarchy of God, there are no little, medium, or big sins. All of us are imperfect. All are unworthy. All are in need of the Cross.

There's a church hymn I have loved since childhood. When-ever I hear its refrain, I can close my eyes and hear my mother's pure soprano voice gracing each note with glorious precision. I can also hear my Grandma Bonnie's voice as well. And while not nearly as pure and perfect pitched as my mother's, Grand-ma Bonnie's voice was still lovely as she sang with unadulter-ated abandon to the One her soul loved. The words to that song still ring in my consciousness:

"WHEN I SURVEY THE WONDROUS CROSS . . ."
"In the gospel account of St. John, I see many sides of the cross of Jesus. I see the cross of betrayal as Judas took the band of soldiers to arrest Jesus. I see the cross of denial as Peter denied knowing our Lord three times. I see the cross of false accusations that caused Pilate to see Jesus as a threat to his own authority and that of Caesar's. I see the cross of mockery, abandonment, and death as the crowd yelled, 'Crucify him! Crucify him!' and no

one came to his aid. As I survey the cross, it is more than a cross of shame, suffering, and death. It is a cross that brings the saving grace of God. It is a wondrous cross."[5]

"ON WHICH THE PRINCE OF GLORY DIED . . ."

Do you remember the names of our enemy, each one describing the dark and hideous nature of his being? Contrast those with the life-imbuing names of Jesus! He is our Priest-Friend,[6] the Advocate[7] who "is able to save forever those who draw near to God through Him, since He always lives to make intercession for them."[8] He is "God's Yes, the Faithful and Accurate Witness, the First of God's creation."[9] Jesus is the Author and Perfecter of Faith,[10] the Bearer of Sin,[11] the Beginning and the End,[12] and True God and Real Life.[13] This is the Prince of Glory who willingly gave his life for you and me and the One who longs to free us from our sin.

"MY RICHEST GAIN I COUNT BUT LOSS . . ."

What is your most treasured gain: a doctorate degree, children, your pristine reputation, or spiritual understanding? What can't you imagine *not* caring about as much? The apostle Paul, whom we've become well acquainted with these past few chapters, says, "You know my pedigree: a legitimate birth, circumcised on the eighth day; an Israelite from the elite tribe of Benjamin; a strict and devout adherent to God's law; a fiery defender of the purity of my religion, even to the point of persecuting Christians; a meticulous observer of everything set down in God's law Book. The very credentials these people are waving around as something special, I'm tearing up and throwing out with the trash—along with everything else I used to take credit for. And why? Because of Christ."[14]

"AND POUR CONTEMPT ON ALL MY PRIDE . . ."

"Yes, all things I once thought were so important are gone from my life. Compared to the high privilege of knowing Christ Jesus as my Master, firsthand, everything I once thought I had going for me is insignificant—dog dung."[15] You gotta love this man, even if his earthy reference to dog poo makes you a little nervous! How I yearn to learn from Paul, who came to understand so deeply the "all-or-nothing" magnificence of Christ. While I'm sure I'm far from counting "everything" as loss, I'm working at it.

"SEE FROM HIS HEAD, HIS HANDS, HIS FEET . . . "

Oh the maternal sorrow and womb-aching agony that must have ripped through Mary, the mother of Jesus, as she saw the head, "a ruined face, disfigured past recognition,"[16] of her beloved son. I cannot fathom her thoughts as she watched the brutal spikes pierce through the skin and sinew, the muscle and bone of her son. The same hands she had protectively held as he took his first tentative steps as a toddler. The same young hands his earthly father, Joseph, had taught to plane wood and create strong dovetailed joints. Those hands, now coursing with blood, had made mud with spit and dirt, covered the eyes of a blind man, and gave him his sight! Those hands had touched the untouchables (lepers, as well as whores and tax men) and offered communion to his disciples only a short time before. And his feet, which until a few hours before had still carried the anointing aroma of Mary Magdalene's sacrifice,[17] were pierced to the Cross as well.

"SORROW AND LOVE FLOW MINGLED DOWN . . ."

When I survey the wondrous Cross my eyes rest on this verse. There he is. Beaten, bloodied, humiliated, and still . . . through the tears of pain and the depth of a spiritual anguish you and I can never comprehend . . . still yet, he loves. In my mind's eye I see the sorrow in his eyes from taking on his shoulders all the sins of humankind. I see his pain of being separated from his Father because the sins he is carrying mean that he cannot be in God's presence. And I see the love that beams hope into a dark world, even at a time of intense agony.

"DID E'ER SUCH LOVE AND SORROW MEET . . . "

Imagine the scene. Jesus is in intense pain, and yet he asks God to have mercy on us, on behalf of our ignorance.[18] Then he offers redemption to one dying near by him,[19] as well as Life to all those who would come. Note that Jesus' offer is to all—even the thief dying on a cross next to him, but again the choice is up to us. We must choose to come. There were two thieves on crosses next to Jesus—one chose to follow him. The other did not.

"OR THORNS COMPOSE SO RICH A CROWN . . . "

It you want to see some gorgeous, rich jewels, just take a little trip to see the British Crown Jewels sometime. They're on display *(with some mighty stiff guards, I might add)* in an underground vault in The Tower of London, beneath the parade ground in front of Waterloo Barracks. Among them are the Sovereign's Scepter, which holds the largest cut diamond in the world and the Imperial State Crown, used for the coronation of Queen Victoria in 1838. The crown contains 3,000 priceless stones, including the second largest cut diamond in the world. And finally there's the Kohinoor diamond in the crown made in 1937 for the coronation of Elizabeth (Queen Mother), George VI's queen.[20]

But as incredible as these earthly treasures are, they will all pale in comparison to the many crowns Christ will wear someday as King of kings and Lord of lords.[21] You might hear a few "ahs" of wonder inside the Tower of London, but no one falls before the Crown Jewels in reverence. However, on "the day of the Lord" (when Jesus returns to earth to gather his followers), *every* knee will bow to Jesus' righteousness, authority, and honor. What a sight that will be to behold!

"WERE THE WHOLE REALM OF NATURE MINE, THAT WERE AN OFFERING FAR TOO SMALL . . . "

"Look around you: Everything you see is God's—the heavens above and beyond, the Earth, and everything on it."[22]

One of the biggest "arguments" for the existence of God is creation itself. Could a big bang have led, by happenstance, to such intricate, complex creations—from plants to animals to human beings? Careful study has convinced even some atheist scientists that there has to be a Creator—an all-powerful God who cares about order and life.

"LOVE SO AMAZING, SO DIVINE, DEMANDS MY SOUL, MY LIFE, MY ALL."

"So now Israel, what do you think God expects from you? Just this: Live in his presence in holy reverence, follow the road he set out for you, love him, serve God, your God, with everything you have in you . . . live a good life."[23]

God is a "take him or leave him" kind of guy. You can't have God halfway. Either you live in his presence and follow him—or you don't. Again, the choice is yours.

TRADING SPACES TRUTH #2

"Say the welcoming word to God—'Jesus is my Master'—embracing, body and soul, God's work of doing in us what he did in raising Jesus from the dead. That's it."[24]

The wondrous and wonderful Cross of history and Scripture provides the way for you and me, as messes of magnificent proportions, to enter into an eternal love relationship with God the Father. Through his death and resurrection, Christ—the only sinless being to ever walk this earth and "touch flesh" with humans—completed the sacrifice that is necessary for our salvation. He died so we have the option of living eternally with God in heaven.

That's it?! Yep, that's it.

There's nothing you can "do" to gain salvation. No one can live a good enough life to be in the presence of God. The Bible makes it clear that we need only accept Jesus' sacrifice on our behalf: "You're not 'doing' anything; you're simply calling out to God, trusting him to do it for you. That's salvation. With your whole being you embrace God setting things right, and then you say it, right out loud: 'God has set everything right between him and me!'"[25]

I also enjoy reading this truth in another translation: "If you confess with your mouth Jesus as Lord, and believe in your heart that God raised Him from the dead, you shall be saved; for with the heart man believes, resulting in righteousness, and with the mouth he confesses, resulting in salvation."[26]

Once we have chosen to accept the gift of salvation for our inherited sin *(remember the Adam and Eve factor)* as well as the sins that trip us up so easily, another portion of Scripture promises, "If we admit our sins—make a clean breast of them— he won't let us down; he'll be true to himself. He'll forgive our sins and purge us of all wrongdoing."[27] Note it says that first we must confess—we must admit our sins. We must see their seriousness and recognize them not as just mistakes or goofs or oopses, but downright sin. Sins that we have committed against God; sins that keep us separated from God and others.

The redemptive promise found in the book of 1 John shows us that God has the ability and power to completely forgive. There's no limit to his forgiveness. If this is the first time you've committed that sin or the thousandth time makes no difference. You can never exhaust the limits of God's forgiveness. And that's indeed good news to us oh-so-human humans.

"Because of the sacrifice of the Messiah, his blood poured out on the altar of the Cross, we're a free people—free of penalties and punishments chalked up by all our misdeeds. And not just barely free, either. *Abundantly* free!"[28]

And that, my dear girlfriend, is the result of divine scandalous grace and radical redemption!

God delights in bringing a sweeping, radical life change. He truly is in the "restoration" business! But I think we tend to forget the rescuing nature of Jesus' redemption, which is to revolutionize the Eternal through the Cross and to release (i.e.

unshackle, liberate, emancipate) women from the day-to-day sins and battles they face.

Now come on! Who among us couldn't stand to wake up with a deeper sense of freedom from her past and present? And who wouldn't want to experience that change forever and ever? Are you waving your hankies, girls? Just listen to the stories of a few others who waved their hankies:

✳ I never thought I would be writing you this note. Some time ago I decided to trust God with this forgiveness thing and actually prayed he would soften my heart toward my husband. You see, he said and did some incredibly hurtful things during our first four years of marriage, and I came to a point where I honestly hated him. I didn't care if he lived or died. I didn't care if he ever made love to me again—or even if he had sex with someone else. In fact, I once prayed he would have sex with someone else, so I could have a way out of this marriage without looking like the bad guy.

But that didn't happen. Instead I began to notice every time I turned on the radio, picked up a random book, or flipped through a magazine, that my ears and eyes were always fixed on something regarding forgiveness. Well, I can tell you right now that forgiving him was the LAST thing on my mind. Having a root canal without numbing agents would have been a better idea!

Yet, time after time, forgiveness popped up. And then you came to town. Your topic was, of course, "Radical Forgiveness." So I listened, and for the first time in, like, forever, I mulled the idea around in my head for longer than three seconds.

Later, after the weekend was over, I was driving home when I just decided to do it. And I prayed, "Okay, God, I'll forgive him if you'll just show me how." Then lo and behold, he showed me. Not in a big, spectacular way, but through slivers of opportunities. Speaking a kind word to him. Initiating sex after months of playing dead. Zipping him an e-mail in the middle of his work day. And praying, always praying, for God to rescue me from my grudges and hurts and show me how to forgive. I can't tell you one specific moment when "it happened!" For me it was more like a slow and steady marathon—taking one step at a time and keeping my eyes on the finish line all the time.

✳ I have been forgiven of adultery by God and my husband, and there's nothing like this feeling in the world! I often wondered how God could redeem this sinful mess of my life. I asked Jesus to be my Savior when I was nine years old. I was such a "good" kid that I think some of my family were happy (sounds kind of sick, doesn't it? But it's true) when I sinned so publicly. I have learned so much. God is faithful and longsuffering, and he can change your heart if you'll listen and do what is right. Since my own restoration I've been able to help other women and to tell them there is hope for change and forgiveness.

✳ I have finally forgiven my mom for breaking our family apart. Nine years ago she disappeared from our family and a 28-year marriage and ran off with another man. Today she's still with him, but they have never married. I have grieved a lot over the last nine years because my mom was my best friend. Each day now I realize that she is missing out on seeing her children's children. But I believe our relationship will one day be restored, and I won't stop praying until it is.

Are you ready for a little *Trading Spaces* action in your own life? Would you like to have a thorough restoration of your sins? To have the rubble of your life carried away and replaced with new material? Like a clean heart, a renewed spirit, or a forgiving attitude?

Are you ready for the Carpenter to enter your home and start renovating? Knocking down walls of your heart, traipsing through your memories, cleaning out closets no one else has looked in, and dusting out from under your mattress? *(Hmm, I've found this Carpenter to be one efficient guy!)* He can reconstruct the rooms of your heart; give you more space to breathe and love than you ever dreamed possible.

Are you prepared to ask God for the seemingly impossible?

Grab a scrap piece of paper that you can write on and then throw away. On that paper write the first name of the LAST person you ever think you can forgive. Next, write the first name of the LAST person you feel can ever forgive you. And one last one—jot down the sin you have said no to the most . . . and then returned to.

Now, I'm going to do a little praying and if you can pipe in with an "amen" every now and then, that would be quite nice.

Here we go (and we're going to pray with our eyes open so you can continue to read the prayer!):

Who do you need to forgive?

> *Lord God, I cannot imagine forgiving* _____*, who has hurt me so badly. You know I can list their offenses right now if I like. How well I know them! I have/haven't tried to forgive them for a long time. But now I'm simply asking you to help me. Help me to forgive them—and to let go of everything that comes attached. Help me to find radical rescue in this area of my life.*

Good! Now let's pray about the one you've hurt.

Who can't forgive you?

> *Lord God, you know* _____ *has not been able to forgive me. (*Choose one: *I know what I did to hurt them and I am truly sorry for that.* Or, *I don't know what I did to offend them so badly and I don't have to). I'm simply asking you to help them forgive me, even if I don't deserve it. Show them the truth of redemption and of living a life that is freed from all sin, all grudges, and all regrets. And help me to build a bridge of restoration in that relationship if it is healthy to do so and what you desire.*

And uh, what's that sin you keep returning to?

> *Lord God, you know I struggle with* _____*. I have tried to kick that habit in my own power, but it's impossible to do so. This time, God, I am on my knees. I know I can't do it on my*

own. Only with your power can I overcome this sin—and that's what it is. Help me, God. Give me the courage and determination to take the steps I should to stop this sin from controlling my life.

Amen.

Ladies, because Jesus made the choice to become the crux of our redemption, a life of forgiveness is possible. But *only* through Jesus, who made the ultimate sacrifice. There's no other way.

So it all comes down to this one big question: Do you believe that Jesus thought YOU were worth dying for?

Do you really believe that? And if so, are you living like you believe it?

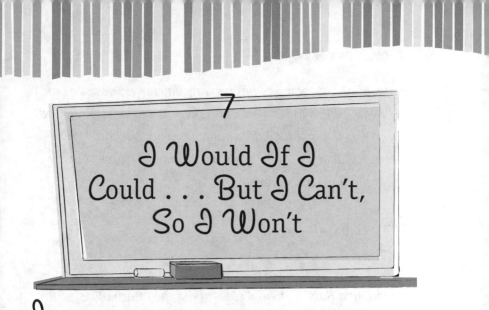

I Would If I Could . . . But I Can't, So I Won't

I can remember thinking when I was young that once I got to be a certain age, everything would be better. *(Déjà vu! You may remember a similar* Scandalous *thought of an 85-year-old woman in the bathroom of Hartsfield International Airport in Georgia!*)*

I imagined that once I graduated from high school, finished college, got married, found a job, and had my own children to love, life would be easy. And I found myself praying as much.

It went something like this at age 8:

> *Dear God,*
> *Today I learned that your Son, Jesus Christ, is going to come back to earth someday. I think that's really cool. But I was hoping you could wait a few more years. I really want to grow up and be a mommy.*

And this, at age 16:

> *Dear God,*
> *My grandma was talking about Jesus returning to earth.*

* See *Scandalous Grace,* pp. 29–31, for a story that will make you laugh, cry, and identify.

*She thinks it's going to happen any day now. She asked me
if I was excited to see you. I told her yes, but you know, God,
that was a minor lie. I do want to see you, but could you
please wait a few more years before sending Jesus? I really
want to have sex someday.*

And this, at age 21:

*Dear God,
I taught a Sunday school class about the return of Jesus. It
really is exciting to think I might actually hear an angel sound
a trumpet announcing your arrival. But you know Rick and
I are engaged to be married. And my wedding dress is going
to be gorgeous, and I'll be able to have sex. (Finally!!!) Do
you think you could wait? Just a while longer?*

And at age 23:

*Dear God,
Thank you for this little one growing inside me! I can't wait
to see who he or she is. Thank you, thank you, thank you for
letting me be a mom! And I was just thinking . . . could you
please have Jesus wait to come back to earth until I have this
baby and all the ones after? I can't wait to hold them all and
be a full-time mommy!*

Then Julie, age 25, mother of two under the age of two:

Come, sweet Jesus!!!!!!

Can any of you identify with me, right now? You see, even when we "arrive" at that next longed-for stage, it's still never quite enough (or maybe, in the case of moms of young children, it's sometimes too much all at once!). And this brings us to another forgiveness fact.

FORGIVENESS 101
Life is filled with contradictions even after salvation.
GLARING REALITY
We sometimes border on the edge of hypocrisy.

You know, it's easy to think that after you make the choice to accept Jesus' sacrifice for you (as we discussed in the "Trading Spaces" chapter) that *presto, chango,* your life will be smooth— no bumps, no hills to climb—from then on. But if I've learned anything thus far in 38 years of living, it's this: Life is not about quick fixes; it's about the process. Some of the same sins may still make your life difficult, even after you've accepted Christ. You may still crave that drink, long for a sexual tryst, or feel anger toward the coworker who's skinnier, smarter, or more well liked than you. You'll still have the same personality quirks, those idiosyncrasies that drove you *(maybe others too)* crazy before. As for me, despite my rather self-centered prayers, I'm still looking forward to seeing Jesus. I just hope he waits until I finish this book deadline! *(Now for sure you've got my personality pegged.)*

We're never "safe" from sin's tempting grip or the past coming back to lure us. The moment you think you are, watch out! Our enemy isn't called the Deceiver for nothing. And it is because we are never safe that we need a Savior. Although we accept Christ once, we have a continuing need, on a day-by-day basis, for the rescuing redemption of Christ that refines our faith, shapes our character, and draws us close, once again, to God.

Redemption's rescue covers the broad range of God's activity in the process of our life as believers in Christ. We *are saved* from the guilt of sin (justification[1]), *are being saved* from the power of sin (sanctification[2]), and *will be saved* from the judgment and presence of sin in the life to come (glorification[3]). The whole of redemption (incorporating all three processes) is to restore us to the original purpose of our creation—to love God, worship him, and enjoy him forever.*

A large part of making this radical step toward redemption is in our admitting we can't do it on our own; in our admitting our constant need for rescue—and for a Savior.

Life may not be what you signed up for. You may feel as though you're still living in the rubble of your past—in the broken, fragmented pieces of past choices, scorched places, current temptations, and future worries. But now is the time to take some proactive steps in cleaning up the rubble and creating something new.

How can you do that?

#1: CALL THINGS WHAT THEY ARE.
Admit what you've done and that you aren't who you claim to be. Let's become truth tellers, ladies. With God, with others, and with the running conversation we have with ourselves day

---

* This portion is taken from the Westminster Confession of Faith written in 1646. What an incredible summation of Christian theology and sound doctrinal truth.

in and day out. Go back to our four-word confession: "I am
a mess" and then let someone else in on the details that need
to be told. *(If you're really feeling gutsy, then add the next three
words too: "of magnificent proportions"!)*

Listen to what this gutsy woman revealed on her survey:

Jhe best thing I ever did was admit my addiction to Internet porn
sites. I told my husband, if you can believe it! I know most stories
talk about the man being the one with the problem, but it was me.
Admitting my sin and telling my husband how difficult it was for me
to stop, even though I wanted to, strengthened my love for him and
has helped me break away from the lure of fantasies and sin.

That's a tough thing for any person to admit, so whoever you
are, I admire your courage . . . and I'm on the sidelines cheering
you on as you continue your journey.

You see, in order to start any process of healing, you first
have to strip away the labels (i.e., codependency) that say it's
okay to be what you are. Next you must take the steps you need
to face your sin. Do you need to attend AA? Get counseling?
Or find a friend who will have the guts to hold you accountable,
even when you start to get angry?

Don't allow excuses to hinder redemption's work in you.
Until you recognize your part in the problem and acknowledge
it, you won't get anywhere.

#2: TAKE THE WORD REPENT SERIOUSLY.
Repent isn't just a term used by old fogeys. Repent means a
turning back, saying you're sorry and meaning it. It means that

you ask God to forgive you and to help you not commit that same sin again. It also means you admit to God that you've been rebelling against him but are now ready to walk away from your sin. *(And you're not going to leave any trap doors or back entrances to get back in, either.)*

A believer does not have to sin. But we still do. We allow the deceit of sin to creep into our mind. We reason, *It's not that bad.* Or, *No one will ever know.* Or, the queen of excuses: *Everyone does that anyway.* We crave the power of the flesh (sin offers pleasure sexually, mentally, and physically). And we sometimes purposefully claim a lack of knowledge regarding God's instructions for guiding us out of sin.[4] But the deceit of sin only clouds our judgment and keeps us bound.

Repentance not only involves our turning from specific sins but also changing our attitudes, thinking, speech, and actions. It's about living in *Jesus!* "You received Christ Jesus, the Master; now *live* him. You're deeply rooted in him. You're well constructed upon him. You know your way around the faith. Now do what you've been taught. School's out; quit studying the subject and start *living* it! And let your living spill over into thanksgiving."[5]

What's keeping you from acting in repentance? Are you ready to start living it? I mean, *really* living it?

If so, you're ready for the next step.

#3: BEGIN TO REBUILD YOUR FOUNDATIONS OUT OF THE RUBBLE, WITH GOD'S HELP.

Who wants to believe how much rubble they have in their life, much less start a reconstruction project with it? But it's only

when you admit you have rubble and decide you don't want
it cluttering up your life anymore that you can start rebuilding
a solid foundation, rather than a shaky one.

I had to face the fact that I'd built piles of rubble as a result
of my angry past—and admit that what I'd constructed certainly
wasn't pretty. All those consequential remnants were piled so
high it took a long time for me even to imagine climbing over
them. Broken pieces of my heart, my home, and my dreams
appeared all but impossible to repair. But God revels in the
impossible.

And that's a good thing!

An amazing thing!

A radical thing!

With his help, I began to crawl over my rubble, bit by bit. Up
and over the boulder of my adoptive past—finally acknowledg-
ing the fact that I'd always felt "given away" by my birth mother.
Then through the rubble of regret—finally letting go of the fact
that I couldn't remember her face or anyone else in my birth
family, except for the two sisters who lived with me for a brief
time in foster care. Step by step, sometimes inch by inch, I
made my way up, over, around, beneath, and through the past
and the consequences of my actions. Once I gained some
insight on dealing with my anger and verbal explosions, I had
to work hard to rebuild my children's trust. I had to do the same
thing with my husband financially, after years of lying about
how much I spent until the ugly and cumulative damage was
revealed.

Was the process easy? No, it was downright painful. And
I'm still working on some of those areas. But rebuilding your

foundations is possible. I needed to learn where I stood and what counted most in my life in order to be able to see God's priorities for my life.

#4: START LIVING IN TRUTH—IN THE LIGHT OF GOD'S SCANDALOUS GRACE.

God graciously built out of the scandalous fragments of my past an incredible opportunity to speak to other mothers—out of my weakness and his proven strength—and proclaim that nothing is impossible for him.

But first I had to come clean about my sin before he could forgive me and give me a heart of restored tenderness and joy for my children. I had to ask my husband to intervene when I was beginning to lose it with the kids. And he did.

Even further, God put me where I never thought I'd be. I had to research information for a book idea, write a proposal, meet deadlines *(which I can have quite a difficult time with!)*, and do the work of a writer, all the while meeting the demands of home and family. Then God graciously allowed the book to fall into the hands of all who needed to read its message.

And ladies, the feedback has been astounding. I say this not to toot my own horn, but because I was extremely humbled to know just how many of you have struggled—or are struggling— with the same things I do. How affirming it has been to me that we women truly are all sisters. Sisters who need God's scandalous grace and his radical forgiveness! Sisters who need to extend that same grace and radical forgiveness not only to each other, but to ourselves, as well!

Girlfriends, now is the time to embrace the fact that *nothing* is unreachable. With God, all things indeed are possible.[6] Radical forgiveness can take you to all the previously unreachable places on a journey, but YOU have to go along. You need to do whatever you can to assist the process, instead of dragging your heels, saying, "This is just too hard" or "Maybe it's not so bad after all."

When the work gets hard, keep in mind: This life may not always make sense now, but someday it's all going to work! And that's why we can look forward to the exquisite hope of heaven!

#5: RETURN DAILY TO THE CROSS AND YOUR NEED FOR CHRIST (SEE THE "TRADING SPACES" CHAPTER).

Ask God what to do not only today, but every day. Not only on Sunday, but on Monday, Tuesday, Wednesday, Thursday, Friday, and even Saturday. The reason for the Cross is that God knew how desperately you'd need it. You weren't even on this earth 2,000 years ago. But all your sins—past, present, future, and even the ones you commit over and over—were covered with that one magnificent act of sacrifice and love. That act was all-inclusive, for all eternity. And it is yours for the asking.

But it still sounds too easy, doesn't it? Like a magical formula of "Bippity, boppety, boo" and our life is fixed. But we can never escape the consequences of our sins, whether in the past or in the present. And that sobering thought is what should push us on to a different kind of life.

"So, since we're out from under the old tyranny, does that mean we can live any old way we want? Since we're free in the freedom of God, can we do anything that comes to mind? Hardly. You know well enough from your own experience that there are some acts of so-called freedom that destroy freedom. Offer yourselves to sin, for instance, and it's your last free act. But offer yourselves to the ways of God and the freedom never quits. All your lives you've let sin tell you what to do. But thank God you've started listening to a new master, one whose commands set you free to live openly in *his* freedom!"[7]

The scandalous and radical reality is that God not only sent his Son, Jesus, to die for your sin, but that he continues to forgive you every time for every sin.

God is there to fix the scorched places, those places that bring continual pain and deep soul hurt. Will you let him?

He's also there to fix the "little messes"—the simple, predictable things that bug you and bring you down. The little things that you fall into on a regular basis, as much as you try not to.

But you have a part too—you have to choose not to remain stuck in the rut. Apart from God's help, you cannot help yourself. No self-help book in the world will be enough self-help. The old adage is true: Hope deferred *can* make the heart sick.[8] But you're the one who can choose either to stay heartsick and stuck in your rut—or choose to look at the larger picture. Most of you have at least heard of the "Serenity Prayer":

> *God grant me the serenity*
> *to accept the things I cannot change;*
> *courage to change the things I can;*
> *and wisdom to know the difference.*

What people usually don't know is the rest of this prayer, by 20th-century theologian Reinhold Niebuhr, that brings everything into an even sharper perspective:

> *Living one day at a time;*
> *Enjoying one moment at a time;*
> *Accepting hardship as the pathway to peace.*
> *Taking, as He did, this sinful world*
> *as it is, not as I would have it. . . .*
>
> *Trusting that He will make all things right*
> *if I surrender to His will.*
> *That I may be reasonably happy in this life*
> *and supremely happy with Him forever in the next.*[9]

The truth is, each of us wants *complete* satisfaction and fulfillment right now, right here. But it's not going to happen. It can't happen. I believe that vague "not yet" tugging is part of God's redemptive plan. It points us to what lies ahead and lights a fire under us of exquisite hope for the future and our secure placement in his arms.

A powerful scene in the last book of The Lord of the Rings trilogy imbues the redemptive truths we speak of. In it a contrite Hobbit, named Pippin, has been caught gazing into a forbidden sphere. And what he sees puts his life in grave danger. Within a matter of moments those around him scurry to deal with the inevitable consequences of his actions, and he realizes he's forced to leave his beloved friend, Merry. Standing silent, Pippin watches as those around him prepare for war.

It is the cost of his rebellion, and Pippin understands this. Then, just as he makes eye contact with Merry and it feels as though Pippin will bear the weight of his guilt alone, the powerful hooves of Gandalf's steed are heard. And, faster than lightning, the white horse charges by Pippin, and the powerful arm of Gandalf reaches low and scoops the Hobbit from his feet. And then . . . oh then! . . . Gandalf places Pippin firmly against his chest, lays a protective arm across him, and sets his gaze toward what lies ahead.

I wept during that movie scene. My 14-year-old son "got it" too. But my 9-year-old and my husband just looked at me like I was crazy. Oh! The image of that guilty Hobbit—frail and frightened, being embraced and held by his protector and friend . . . well, it sent chills down my spine. And I said out loud, "I get it! I really get it!"

This is the tale of redemption.

You and I standing silent in our guilt and regret.

Unable to fix what we've done.

Gazing at the ones we have lost as a result of our guilt.

Alone.

Afraid.

And then our Protector swoops in!

With glorious abandon he rides . . . his gaze fixed on you.

You. Standing there. In need of help.

Then lovingly he bends low (the very meaning of grace!), sweeps you off your feet, and firmly, yet tenderly, places you protectively against his chest. He fixes his eyes on the future . . . and moves full steam ahead, with you right on the horse with him.

To live a redemptive life is not to live recklessly, but righteously. God can do the impossible, but you have to be willing. You have to embrace and admit your humanity! God says to you, "We're going to fix what's wrong in your life . . . but you're going with me."

That means you can't sit in the audience and watch how the scene is being played out. You must choose to participate—to play an active role. And if you do, you will feel the radical excitement of being swept up in his arms and carried all along the way.

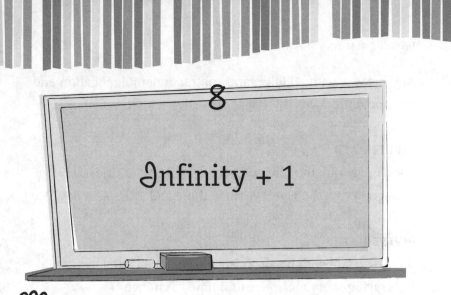

8

Infinity + 1

My composite score for the individual mathematics portion of the ACT college entrance exam was nine.

Yes, I typed and you read the number nine.

Nine out of a possible 33.

Now, if I were the sort of woman to blame others for her shortcomings *(which, of course, I am not)* I would naturally be inclined to mention my seventh-grade math teacher, Ms. Claire Saucier (last name pronounced, "So-see-aaaa."), who suffocated any gasp of interest for things mathematical during the 1977–1978 "New Math" school year.

But enough of such hypothetical ramblings.

I think you get the picture. Let's just say I'm "not so good" with math—and that includes digits, inches, liters, milliliters, or centipedes. On the bright side, if you borrow money from me, I will, in all likelihood, forget I ever gave it to you. And the dark side? Well, if I borrow money from you, I will, in all likelihood, come back for more. *(Since those numbers in my checkbook have such difficulty adding up and all!)*

However, God is excellent with numbers. Fortunate for us!

And his way with addition and subtraction, multiplication and division, introduces the concept of Divine Math.

DIVINE MATH

"Don't overlook the obvious here, friends. With God, one day is as good as a thousand years, a thousand years as a day."[1]

DIVINE MATH

"God isn't late with his promise as some measure lateness. . . . He's giving everyone space and time to change."[2]

DIVINE MATH

"If someone drags you into court and sues for the shirt off your back, giftwrap your best coat and make a present of it. . . . No more tit-for-tat stuff. Live generously."[3]

DIVINE MATH

"Don't hoard treasure down here where it gets eaten by moths and corroded by rust or—worse!—stolen by burglars. Stockpile treasure in heaven, where it's safe from moth and rust and burglars."[4]

DIVINE MATH

"Look at it this way. If someone has a hundred sheep and one of them wanders off, doesn't he leave the ninety-nine and go after the one? And if he finds it, doesn't he make far more over it than over the ninety-nine who stay put? Your Father in heaven feels the same way. He doesn't want to lose even one of these simple believers."[5]

During the summertime, while growing up, I attended Sunday night church services at the Church of God Holiness with my grandparents. Everyone was referred to as "Brother" or "Sister," followed by the last name. For example, Brother Pugh was the pastor. And dear Sister Claysburg's teased and sprayed hairdo nearly knocked out six bulbs in a dangling light fixture. *(I know— I watched them come "this" close . . . and snickered, just a little.)* That woman certainly had "heavenly" hair—high and unto heaven!

It was the mid 70s, and Michael W. Smith had yet to write "Great Is the Lord." Praise and worship music, per se, had yet to arrive in the small Midwest church community of Moberly, Missouri. So I cut my theological teeth on incredible hymn stan-dards such as: "When the Roll Is Called Up Yonder" *(but I was praying for the trumpet of the Lord to wait just a little longer, remember, until I could experience a little more of life),* "Blessed Assurance," "It Is Well," and, of course, "Amazing Grace."

There were no official worship leaders.

Nola played the organ *(if I close my eyes even now, I can hear the "welling up" of that organ),* and someone else attempted to keep up on the piano.

Accompaniment tapes and CDs didn't exist. That meant you were pretty much left to your lonesome whenever singing the "special music" before the offering.

There wasn't a lip-lined mouth, a kohl-lined eye, or a painted fingernail to be found.

There was little to entertain me *(save Sister Clayburg's hairpins, which threatened to fall from her towering hairstyle)* and even less to distract me as I would sit, transfixed, each Sunday evening, listening to others tell how they came to know Jesus.

I miss Testimony Sundays.

I miss hearing the excitement in a new believer's voice.

I miss seeing the tears of mothers and fathers as they listened to their children bravely tell their story of accepting Jesus.

I miss hearing stories of God's faithfulness.

But most of all, I miss hearing a man or woman, boy or girl, tell their church family, "I'm so glad Jesus found me!" For each story bears testimony of the Shepherd's relentless pursuit of that which was lost—of the sheep that had been lost and now was found.

Of the Shepherd gently stooping down to that sheep . . . battered, dirty, limping.

Of the sheep's weak and pitiful baa. Knowing she needs rescue oh, so desperately, but a little ashamed of how she got into this trouble. Wondering why she chose to leave the secure fold in the first place. Realizing that living without the Shepherd wasn't nearly as exciting or freeing as she thought it would be.

And then the kind touch of the Shepherd. The healing touch on her flank. The look of love in his eyes. The warmth of forgiveness. His eyes beckoning—*Come on home, beloved sheep. I've been waiting for you . . . Looking for you. . . .*

Then the sheep, at last willing, allowing herself to be lifted and carried by the Shepherd, over the hills and valleys, through the woods, the muddy pastures, and back to the safety and warmth of the fold.

Such a celebration takes place as that one sheep is restored to the fold!

And so it is as each person is restored to God's fold. Perhaps that's why each and every story I heard on Testimony Sunday brought a catch to my breath and tears to my eyes. For each story (as well as yours and mine) represents the infinite truth of God's grace, hope, and forgiveness.

And that is indeed radical. Because, you see, I know just how human I am. If it were up to me, I'd wait to help someone until I thought they were "deserving" enough. Or I'd leave them wallowing in the mud for a while, to rub it in a little (especially if they'd hurt me in any way). Or I might even rejoice a little in their downfall *(ouch! But true!),* perhaps even sharing *(in a Christian way of course—"pray for So-and-So, because she's struggling with such-and-such")* with another person that sheep's current bad state. Then I'd gather a crowd around me for a magnificent rescue scene. I'd have T.V. cameras and reporters surrounding me as I lifted that person, singlehandedly, from the mud and extended a warm hug of love and forgiveness.

How glad I am that God acts far differently—and quietly. Note in the story of the Shepherd and the Lost Lamb that the Shepherd doesn't gather a crowd around to view the fallen state of the sheep. No one but the Shepherd and the sheep know exactly what condition the sheep was in when she was found. The only thing that matters to the Shepherd is finding that lost sheep. So he drops everything else he is doing and goes quietly himself to gather that sheep and to bring her home.

Remember Buzz Lightyear's famous phrase in the movie *Toy Story*? "To infinity—and beyond!" And that's where God goes. He takes it to that extra measure, goes the extra mile, and is always ready to add one more to his eternal account ledger.

God goes to "Infinity+1."

And that "1" he has in mind is you.

That puts a whole new perspective on things, doesn't it? Yes,

"He's got the whole world in his hands" as the children's song says, but he's also got you, the "1" firmly in view too.

And that's good news for each of us: God always has you on his mind.

You. The woman who is trying to be all things to all people and is dying inside. The woman who struggles to love her husband and is contemplating an affair. The woman who is having difficulty admitting that some days it's just hard to get out of bed. The woman who is grieving a miscarriage. The woman who remembers an abortion, back in her youth—or not so long ago. The woman who betrayed her best friend. The woman who yelled at her kids. The woman who has a secret drinking problem. The woman who is on a crash diet in an attempt to feel good about herself again. The woman who longs for a husband. The woman who has pushed everyone away because of her sarcastic tongue. The woman who experienced childhood abuse. The woman who has physically abused her own children. The woman who undercut a coworker. The woman who gossiped about a hurting soul . . . and found out later how much that hurt.

You. The woman God loves. The woman to whom God extends scandalous grace and radical forgiveness. And he longs for you to know and experience his infinite truths.

INFINITE TRUTH #1
God's forgiveness is all-inclusive.

That means no one—no matter of age, stage, race, background, past mistakes or failures—is excluded from his offer of radical forgiveness.

How can I be so sure of that? The Father of Creation's concern for the whole world is not an occasional theme in Scripture. If you were to read the Bible and simply mark the portions pertaining to evangelism and missions with a red pen, you'd soon have a well-veined map leading straight to the Father's heart. From its genesis moment of creation to time without end—the salvation of the entire world has always been paramount in God's mind.

He chose to do it creatively, as the Creator does. By sending his Son, in human flesh, to walk the earth, to talk with and physically touch the people of that day. And then, after three years of active ministry, recorded in the Gospels, the first four books of the New Testament, Jesus followed his Father's bidding. He chose to die for the sins of the *entire world.* What a heavy burden to bear! No wonder he sweated blood! No one else who has walked the earth in all of history has ever borne the sins of the whole world on his shoulders. And that's what makes the Christian faith so distinct. Not only did Jesus bear the sins of the world—and that includes yours and mine— he died for them. And if that isn't amazing enough to believe, consider this! After Jesus' resurrection, many bodies of believers left their tombs *(yes, they had been dead!),* entered the holy city of Jerusalem, and appeared to many, [6] declaring the truth of Christ.

And then even those who did not believe in him saw him raised from the dead, walking around!

Only Jesus Christ can offer all-inclusive forgiveness through the exclusive work of the Cross. Why?

Because he's uniquely positioned by virtue of *who he is:* "This is how much God loved the world: He gave his Son, his one and only Son."[7]

Because of *what he accomplished:* "If, when we were at our worst, we were put on friendly terms with God by the sacrificial death of his Son, now that we're at our best, just think of how our lives will expand and deepen by means of his resurrection life!"[8]

Through accepting the death of Jesus on the cross on our behalf, you can experience radical forgiveness—and a liberty and freedom as well. (We'll more closely identify and discuss these in the chapter "Wide-Open Spaces.")

INFINITE TRUTH #2
God's forgiveness is permanent.

For me, this image describes it best: "As far as the east is from the west, so far has He removed our transgressions from us."[9] And that's an infinite distance apart! It means God accomplishes the impossible. He removes your sins an infinite distance from you.

We read in Isaiah 38:17, "In your love you kept me from the pit of destruction; you have put all my sins behind your back" (NIV). God's love keeps us from being destroyed, ladies! Even as bad as it may seem sometimes or how bad it feels even right now, you are not "destroyed." God will not allow the Devil—the Prince of all lies, darkness, and destruction—to destroy you. God even chooses to do something more. When you accept the work of God's Son on the Cross, God puts your sins somewhere that you can't even see them—behind his own back! Think about that a little more. If your sins are behind God's back, it means even he is choosing not to see those sins anymore. Now how's that for radical, permanent forgiveness?

So why is it that we sometimes continue to sin? Ahh, now there's the crux of the issue and our humanness. Somehow we decide we need that sin back—at least to see what it looked like—so we, figuratively speaking, sneak behind God's back and take that sin out again. . . . We'll talk more about that later.

Also check out Isaiah 43:25, where God declares, "But I, yes I, am the one who takes care of your sins—that's what I do. I don't keep a list of your sins."[10] Another translation of that same verse reads, "I, even I, am the one who *wipes out* your transgressions for My own sake; and I *will not remember your sins*"[11] (italics mine).

But how do we know God won't take that sin out and look at it again? Because God never breaks his promise. Scripture declares that boldly. Just take a look at a few:

God has done what he said he would do: I have succeeded David my father and ruled over Israel just as God promised; and now I've built a Temple to honor God, the God of Israel. —*1 Kings 8:20*

Let's keep a firm grip on the promises that keep us going. He always keeps his word. —*Hebrews 10:23*

Everything that goes into a life of pleasing God has been miraculously given to us by getting to know, personally and intimately, the One who invited us to God. The best invitation we ever received! We were also given absolutely terrific promises to pass on to you—your tickets to participation in the life of God after you turned your back on a world corrupted by lust. —*2 Peter 1:3-4*

God isn't late with his promise as some measure lateness. He is restraining himself on account of you, holding back the End because he doesn't want anyone lost. He's giving everyone space and time to change. —*2 Peter 3:9*

And his Word is a rock-solid guarantee.

"God *can't* break his word. And because his word cannot change, the promise is likewise unchangeable."[12] "And this is the promise which He [God] Himself made to us: eternal life."[13]

You can't get any more permanent than *forever.* This infinite truth should have us dancing on our feet and whooping and hollering! The God of the Universe *forgives* and—even more amazing—*forgets* the sin and willful rebellion that you and I have confessed! And then he offers us eternal life and a place in heaven, right by his side! Talk about the perfect forever home *(bet there's no dust bunnies to clean in heaven, either)*!

INFINITE TRUTH #3
God's forgiveness isn't a onetime thing. He forgives time and time again.

Talk about radical (i.e., *revolutionary—completely and fundamentally changing the "norm"*) infinite truth. This is it.

God doesn't sit on his heavenly throne and say, "You again? What now!"

And he doesn't sigh and say, "I'm so sick of hearing from

YOU. Get lost!" *(Isn't that what we tend to do if someone approaches us, time and time again, for forgiveness?)*

God doesn't roll his eyes and throw the "L" (loser) sign up on his forehead when he hears you pray yet again, "God, please forgive me. I messed up again. I just don't know what's wrong with me. I do what I don't what to do, and I don't do what I should do." [14] Sound familiar? Even Paul, who had come so far (from the Christian-killer Saul to become the apostle Paul), admitted he just couldn't do it right sometimes either. *(Now there's a relief!)*

How grateful I am that God knows what to do with messes— and that includes us, as well as the messes we make! One of my favorite "messy authors" Anne Lamott summed it up best: "But there wasn't a single thing that I'd do that Jesus would say, 'Forget it, you're out, I've had it with you, try Buddha!' "[15]

When you accept Jesus' work on the Cross, you are redeemed for all eternity. You need not ask again and again and again for God to save you every time you mess up. Once you admit you are a sinner, you proclaim Jesus as God's Son, you accept that he died on the cross on your behalf, and ask God to forgive you for your sins, you are part of God's family. God accepts you as his own, his child.

But that doesn't mean you pray "The Sinner's Prayer" and *poof!* You instantly become perfect. *(Oh, how I wish it did. It would certainly make my life easier!)* No, day-by-day sins will still pester you. Some days will be good; others will be hard.

The reality is this: As long as we are on this earth, day by day we are also being redeemed. From all those sins that still pester us. From all the guilt, all the remorse, all the anger.

The Cross doesn't take away our human nature, but it takes away our eternal consequences since Christ paid those.

All of us need help from God on a day-by-day basis *(for me, make that moment-to-moment)*. That means even when you disappoint yourself, you can turn back to God. He will listen and help, time and time again.

INFINITE TRUTH #4
God is relentless and crazy about YOU.

During one of the worst times his country had ever experienced, the bombing of London in World War II, the great British states-man Winston Churchill once got up to give what the audience expected to be a very long speech. He leaned over the platform, and then with intensity, simply said, "Never give up. Never, never, never give up!" And then he left the platform.

Well, God is the ultimate example of never, never, never giving up!

Psalm 139 talks about how well God knows us—from the first moment of conception all the way through our present thoughts and actions! We can never outrun, outwit, or outgive God.

He assures us, through his Word, that we can never exhaust his forgiveness. Here's the promise: "If we admit our sins—make a clean breast of them—he won't let us down; he'll be true to himself. He'll forgive our sins and purge us of all wrong-doing."[16]

Now that's a promise I need—all the way to "Infinity + 1!"

9

Forgive and Forget?
. . . and Other Myths

* I bet you've never heard a story such as the one I'm about to tell. When I was three years old, I watched my father kill my mother. My mom and dad had a lot of problems, and everyone in our family and community assumed she took her own life. And I suppose in one way she did. She did pull the trigger. But what no one else has ever known is that I listened to my father goad her on that evening. I heard him yell at her and tell her she was worthless. I snuck a peek around my bedroom door and saw him standing in the living room (she was in the kitchen) and he never moved toward her. He never reached out to help her. He simply mocked her and laughed. Then the gun fired and my dad's mocking laughter turned into screams as he yelled for me to stay in my room. My dad killed my mom as surely as if he'd pulled the trigger himself.

* My stepdad (I can't bring myself to write "father") abused me in every way possible for four years.

✳ My mom abandoned me when I was two. She married a man who wouldn't accept me. My grandmother raised me. She always took me to see my mother but I never called her "mom." I grew up bitter toward her and blamed her for every mistake and problem in my life.

Sigh. You need to know something, ladies. When I wrote *Scandalous Grace,* I fairly raced through chapters and paragraphs. I couldn't stop the flow of words and had story after clever story that I wanted to put down on the page. In fact, I turned in my manuscript nearly two months ahead of schedule.

I had no reason to believe *Radical Forgiveness* would be any different.

But *Radical* was different—*Radical* IS different.

Scandalous peeled back the veneer of our insecurities. *Radical* sandblasts them.

Scandalous leads us to soothing grace. *Radical* leads us to the Cross, where grace was nailed; a tomb where grace was buried; and a resurrection morning, when grace was completed forever and forever.

Radical is not merely my story—*Radical* is the aching, broken story of each of us.

I've stared for hours at my computer screen, all the while speaking aloud, "What do you know about this kind of loss? Even your own insecurities about being adopted don't hold a candle to this type of pain. What do you have to say to a woman who has known this level of betrayal and fear?"

Those questions led me down a trail of careful research, and as a result, I am forever indebted to Lewis B. Smedes for his thorough study of forgiveness. A plethora of facts, quotes, and interviews are available online regarding Mr. Smedes' studies, as well as found in the many books he has written on the subject.

No author has all the answers.

No author can fix all your problems.

But I have found his insightful wisdom to be an instrument of teaching and healing in my own life. I especially encourage you to read *Forgive and Forget: Healing the Pain You Don't Deserve.* This is my personal favorite and will more than make up whatever I may leave unspoken or unaddressed in this one short chapter. Forgiveness indeed is a lifelong journey that cannot be summed up in one book *(as much as authors hope it can and try to make it so!).*

We've talked a lot in this book about your responsibility for decisions that you make in your life. But there are times when the sin you struggle with is a result of someone else's bad action—when a sin has been perpetrated against you (e.g., childhood abuse, a parent abandoning you, a husband walking out, etc.).

If you were sexually abused, you may struggle with forming relationships with the opposite sex or even the same sex. You don't trust anyone not to hurt you. Or you may even be living life recklessly because you feel unclean and unworthy.

If your father or mother walked out when you were young, you may be holding on too tightly to a relationship you have. Because you fear losing another person in your life, you accomplish just that—you smother that person until he or she indeed does leave.

Many of us have every "right" to be bitter, angry, or filled with hate.

Many of us carry around labels of shame and worthlessness—handed to us by those we should have been able to trust. Those who should have loved us but instead undercut our very soul.

Many of us, if given the opportunity to defend our sin, could convince a jury with the overwhelming "this wasn't fair" and "I didn't deserve this to happen" realities of our stories.

But no matter how "right" it may seem to hold on to our anger, our bitterness, our hate, it is never the right thing to do.

Never?

Never.

Do you recall the chief aim of the enemy of our soul? It is to lie, to steal, and to destroy. Choosing not to forgive will destroy your life.

Now that may take time. It may not happen in a day, a week, or even a year or two. But little by little, grudge by grudge, bitter place by bitter place your heart, your mind, your thoughts, your intentions, your memories, as well as your future, will be consumed by the raging flames of a hardened, unforgiving heart.

Often forgiveness is a matter of one or more of the following:

- ✳ **I WON'T** (I refuse to let go of what happened and my feelings toward it);
- ✳ **I CAN'T** (too much hurt has happened; I don't know if I can get past it, or how);
- ✳ **I DON'T** want to (I want to stay in my pain. Even more so, the other person doesn't deserve my forgiveness; he deserves my full revenge).

And we need to move past that step to being willing to forgive
. . . if for no other reason than to be free ourselves.

If for no other reason than to live!

✳ ✳ ✳

How does Satan keep us trapped in unforgiveness? By giving us
a host of false facts that we start to believe are true. Facts that
keep us saying, "I'm not ready yet because . . ."

FALSE FACT #1
Forgiving means ignoring the past and pretending it never
happened.
FORGIVENESS FACT #1
Forgiving doesn't mean blindly forgetting.

In a *Discipleship Journal* article, well-known psychologist and
therapist Dan Allender said: "True forgiveness doesn't mean
releasing your angry feelings and pretending the harm never
happened."[1]

Forgiveness doesn't mean you throw out the platitude lightly,
"Of course I forgive that person. It happened so long ago, I can
barely remember it. I'm sure he or she's changed." Does ignoring the past really help us deal with the pain long-term? Certainly it's easier in the short-term. And it sounds so sweet and
"Christian" to say, "I forgive you."

But that's a false view of forgiveness. Forgiveness doesn't
mean "cutting your losses" or ignoring that the pain of the past
happened. It doesn't mean keeping busy enough so you won't
have time to think about what happened. If you are honest with

yourself, you know, deep in your core, that particular event of hurt *did* happen, and you need to deal with it, not just stuff it in a laundry basket and shut the door. But you also don't need to take the laundry basket out continually, lift each sin out, and keep smelling each dirty item in front of the other person. All dirty laundry needs washing. And all emotional, mental, physical, and psychological laundry requires forgiveness—*your* forgiveness.

Does forgiving mean blindly forgetting and letting life go on, as if there was never any dirty laundry in the closet? Definitely not. Forgiveness is never "looking the other way," or acting as if no wrong has been committed. Forgiving is not excusing the inexcusable, tolerating the intolerable, nor sweeping things under the proverbial carpet. That is NOT God's way.

"I don't think the way you think [God says]. The way you work isn't the way I work. . . . For as the sky soars high above earth, so the way I work surpasses the way you work, and the way I think is beyond the way you think."[2]

God calls a spade a spade, but he opens his arms to forgive us, time and time again. We need to do likewise.

Again, Smedes helps me crystallize my thoughts. The tough truth is, forgiving isn't forgetting. When we forgive someone, we do not forget the hurtful act, as if forgetting came along with the forgiveness package, the way strings come with a violin. If you forget, you will not forgive at all. You can never forgive people for things you have forgotten about. You need to forgive precisely because you have not forgotten what someone did; your memory keeps the emotional pain alive long after the actual hurt has passed.

Forgetting, in fact, may be a dangerous way to escape the inner surgery of the heart that we call forgiving. There are two kinds of pain that we forget. We forget hurts too trivial to bother about. We forget pains too horrible for our memory to manage. Once we have forgiven, however, we get a new freedom to forget. This time forgetting is a sign of health; it is not a trick to avoid spiritual surgery. We *can* forget *because* we have been healed.

But even if it is easier to forget after we forgive, we should not make forgetting a *test* of our forgiving. The test of forgiving lies with healing the lingering pain of the past, not with forgetting that the past ever happened. The really important thing is that we have the power to forgive what we *still* do remember.

FALSE FACT #2
You can hurt those who hurt you by refusing to forgive.
FORGIVENESS FACT #2
You're the one who hurts if you refuse to forgive.

What happens to the one who sinned against you when you refuse to forgive?

Sad to say, often nothing, at least on the surface. If you're still around that person, she may notice that you're more "icy," or he may notice you don't talk unless you absolutely have to when you're around him. But chances are, unless that person repents (turns their sinful ways around and decides to do life differently) and asks your forgiveness, they won't have a soft enough conscience to care whether you forgive them or not. For them it's all "no big deal"—"water under the bridge." And they haven't seen any consequences yet. (But they will have consequences since God says that anything you do to another will come back to you. Note that God doesn't say, "*Maybe* what you sow, you *may* reap." He's clear-cut about consequences: "You *will* reap what you sow." And what you do will be revealed and judged, in the end.)

But what happens to you when you fail to forgive?

Ahh . . . now the results are far different. Watch how subtly the changes happen, until you become a person you don't want to be. As one woman told me when speaking about the man who had hurt her, "I've hated him for so long that I don't know how not to hate anymore."

A hardness, an anger, a resentment develops that will poison all of your relationships—including your relationship with God. Then you will only want revenge. Such thoughts of revenge can take over every aspect of your life. And you may end up sinning even more, because of that hate and desire to get even.

Consider this: What was done to you was horrible, hurtful, painful. But in God's mathematical equation (see the chapter "Infinity + 1") there are no "degrees" of sin. There are no granddaddy or baby sins. No ranking on a chart. Gossip (slandering another's reputation) and anger are on the same par as murder; lusting over another's spouse is the same as physically having sex with a person who isn't your spouse. That means if you break God's law once (and what person has walked the earth, other than Jesus, who hasn't sinned in some way?) you're guilty of breaking all of his law (not just one teensy part—see James 2:10). Romans 6:23 says that the wages of ALL sin is death because sin means separation from God, the Source of life.

God sees the issue of forgiveness in relating to others as a very serious issue. "For if you forgive men when they sin against you, your heavenly Father will also forgive you. But if you do not forgive men their sins, your Father will not forgive your sins" (Matthew 6:14-15, NIV). Wow—that hits me right between the eyes because I so want and need to be forgiven for all the things I do wrong myself!

Yes, forgiving is costly. But refusing to forgive is even more costly. It can lead to all sorts of physical and emotional ailments, including stomach ulcers, headaches, fits of anger, waves of depression, etc. So when you think you're punishing the other person, think again. You're really punishing yourself!

So what are your other choices? Not a blind, lightweight "I forgive you." Not a "I'm going to get you, my pretty . . . and your little dog too" kind of revenge. Instead, you can choose to "overcome evil with good" (Romans 12:21, NASB).

Sounds crazy, doesn't it? But it's the scandalous dichotomy of the divine. If you want to be first, you have to be last.

God is in the business of making the weak strong. It's because of his crazy, scandalous grace, his radical redemption and forgiveness, and the exquisite hope Jesus brings that you can choose not only not to further the evil, but to halt the cycle of evil right there.

No, that person doesn't deserve forgiveness—God's or yours. But then again, neither do you.

FALSE FACT #3

If you forgive those who hurt you, they'll get off scot-free. No consequences.

FORGIVENESS FACT #3

Forgiveness doesn't mean letting the other person do the same thing to you again.

1 Corinthians 13:4-5 says: "Love . . . doesn't keep score of the sins of others." But some of us want to make sure we not only keep score, but we keep that scoreboard handy so we can continually review it. Because if the scoreboard gets lost, the other person gets off with no consequences and goes happily free. And we certainly wouldn't want that! Even thinking about it makes the steam come out of our ears!

But is that what forgiveness means? The person reaps no consequences for their sin? Again, not in God's plan. Galatians 6:7 explains quite clearly, "Don't be misled: No one makes a fool of God. What a person plants, he will harvest."[3]

Forgiving doesn't mean, as we discussed earlier, a blind forgiveness. There will be consequences for sinful actions—whether now or in the future. You may not be able to trust that person ever again since trust is something earned. And there are some situations (for example, abuse) where you should take measures never to be alone with that person again, if it is within your power to guard against it.

The larger picture of forgiveness is this: Forgiving someone who betrayed you means that you have taken the reins—you have decided to let go of the hurt, the anger, the fear, the bitterness. And that you have decided to go in a different direction instead of letting the person or situation control your life. Some relationships cannot be fixed—nor should they be fixed.

Look at it this way. With God, there is no such thing as unconditional forgiveness. Surprised? Especially since you hear often that God's love for us is unconditional? His love, yes. His forgiveness, no. For God's forgiveness of our sins is grounded in the conditional sacrifice of Christ on the Cross and his resurrection from the dead.[4] First John 2:12 (NIV) says: "your sins have been forgiven on account of his name."

The benefits of this divine forgiveness are available upon the condition that men or women acknowledge their wrongful behavior and status as lost sinners. In other words, they need to repent. And not the kind of light "I'm sorry. I won't do it again" just to get them off the hook, so they can take a breather and then commit that same sin again. Instead they must truly repent—choose a different direction for their actions. And then they must follow through in that different direction, with God's help.

Lewis Smedes hits it on the head when he notes:*

FORGIVING IS NOT TOLERANCE.

$\mathcal{F}$orgive me and you heal yourself. Tolerate everything I do and you are in for a lot of trouble. You can forgive someone almost anything. But you cannot tolerate everything.

$\mathcal{W}$henever people try to live or work together, they have to decide on the sorts of things they will put up with. Every group has to decide what it will put up with and what it cannot tolerate. But what we need to remember is this: **We don't have to tolerate what people *do***

* Lewis Smedes' material has been adapted from online sources: www.http://withchrist.org/forgive.htm

just because we forgive them for doing it. Forgiving heals us personally. To tolerate everything only hurts us all in the long run.

FORGIVING IS NOT EXCUSING.

*E*xcusing is just the opposite of forgiving. We excuse people when we understand that **they were NOT to blame.** Excusing is easy; forgiving is tough. What a mistake it is to confuse forgiving with being mushy, soft, gutless, and oh, so understanding. Before we forgive, we stiffen our spine, and we **hold a person accountable.** Only then, in tough-minded judgment, can we do the outrageously impossible thing: We can forgive.

FORGIVING IS NOT SMOTHERING CONFRONTATION.

*S*ome people hinder the hard work of forgiveness by smothering confrontation. The tendency starts way back when we were kids—and the fact that many parents, in general, are dedicated to smothering conflict. They shush us and soothe us and assure us that whatever makes us mad is not worth raising a fuss about. They get between us and the rotten kid who did us wrong, always protecting, always pinning down the arms of our rage, forever pacifying. Their "now thens" and "there theres" keep us from ever unloading our anger and from ever forgiving. They say, "Forgive and forget," but what they mean is: "Don't make a fuss. I can't stand the noise." But quieting troubled waters is not the same as rescuing drowning people, and smothering conflict is not the same as helping people to forgive each other.

FALSE FACT #4

You can change him (or her).

FORGIVENESS FACT #4:
You're responsible only for you.

All the *I wishes* in the world cannot change another person. You can be responsible only for yourself. What happened to you may not have been your fault. But in the long run, you are responsible only for *you.* How *you* respond during your own sin and after others sin against you. You are not responsible for what someone else does. Nor are you in the business of changing a person's heart—only God can do that.

So how can you forgive?

Perhaps because we're human, we put it in human terms. Peter thought he was doing well if he forgave someone seven times (see Matthew 18:21). I'm with Peter. Seven times seems like plenty to me. *(In fact, that's being just a little too generous in my book.)* Yet Jesus pushed the figure to 70 times 7, shocking his audience. By using that example, Jesus wasn't trying to make his audience get out their calculators (or fingers, in that day) and do the math. He was simply saying, "Look, guys and gals, there's no limit on forgiveness. Forgive anyone and everyone as often as necessary and make it a lifestyle."

Think that's impossible?

Then just see how your life would change if you did the following:

✳ Decide that you will forgive, even if it seems horribly difficult or impossible to do. Ask God to help you mouth the words, even if you can't feel them.

✳ Treat that sinful person (if still in your life) with compas-
sion *(caveat: unless dangerous to you or your family!)*. Tell
the person you forgive him, but because of his actions,
there are consequences.

✳ Remember that trust—if it can be established—needs
to be rebuilt slowly. Time can be a healer, but it's also
a slow healer.

After his wife had an affair, Marco asked her to do three things
to help rebuild his trust if she really cared about him and their
marriage:

1. Go to counseling with him each week and also have
   a separate counseling appointment herself.
2. Do one thoughtful, loving thing for him each day
   to show that she really cared about continuing their
   relationship.
3. Cut off contact with her "lover," and agree to no longer
   use e-mail or the Internet since cybersurfing is what got
   her in trouble in the first place.

✳ Set up boundaries or parameters to protect yourself and
others, and outline specific steps of action if the behavior
happens again. For example, when one family discovered
that an uncle had sexually molested a neighborhood child,
that uncle was no longer allowed to attend family func-
tions. However, each family member phoned him on a
regular basis, dropped off food, wrote him letters, and

remembered him on holidays. The adults in the family even stopped by occasionally to see him. But under no circumstances was he allowed to be around any children in the family—ever—by himself.

Yes, our self-worth is fragile. We long to be loved and valued. And when someone we love or trust betrays us, we are threatened and hurt to the very core. Developing a heart of forgiveness so we can forgive one another as Christ in God forgave us (see Ephesians 4:32) takes time. And it includes looking at our own detestable self first. There's nothing like realizing your own shortcomings that puts others' sins in perspective.

Is there someone you just can't forgive? It takes courage, integrity, and faith to walk in forgiveness. And it's not easy. But it's the radical path. The one God calls us to. And it's the only road to freedom.

✳ ✳ ✳

What about forgiving God?

How can you make peace when you're angry with God?

A hard truth: Sometimes life hurts us. And when it does, we get angry. If there's no individual to blame, it's natural to blame the One who controls everything—God.

✳ A friend of mine was on the jet that crashed into the World Trade Center North Tower on September 11, 2001. She had just gone back to work after having her second child and was a Christian. But what I can't understand and haven't

been able to resolve (nice word for saying "can't forgive")
is the fact that she prayed about her decision to return
to work and she truly felt she had God's blessing to return
to her job. Explain this to me! Why would God tell my
friend to go back to a job that he knew would kill her?!
Three years have passed and I still miss her so much.
I don't understand why this had to happen any more than
I did at 11:32 A.M. that awful day, when her husband called
and told me she was gone.

✳ I found my eight-month-old daughter dead in her crib. I
had laid her down an hour before—warm, soft, and alive.
I was less than 20 feet from her the entire time. Why
didn't God let me know she was dying?! Why didn't he
nudge her or do something big and powerful like I've
heard other mothers talk about? Why would he want
to take my beautiful baby girl from me?

I recently had a conversation with a woman who'd suffered
three miscarriages during her eight years of marriage and had
yet to have a child, while all her friends already had or were
having babies. Another friend is in chronic back pain because
of a car accident five years ago, when she was hit by a teenager
who had just gotten her license.

All these stories rip at our heart. Every one of us reading
them cannot only sympathize but *empathize*—truly feel their
pain, for we have had similar questions, the same doubts, and
an equal propensity to blame God.

But *has* God done anything wrong? God is sinless, perfect.

If anyone moves away, it is us. We're the one who puts up the barrier between the two of us. And that means for the barrier to be removed, our attitude has to change. God is always willing and able to talk with us. But are we always willing to talk to him?

How many of us have *poo-poohed* the intensity of our own anger, disappointment, and rage toward God?

And how many of us have encouraged a smothering of feelings when we are confronted with a friend who is livid against God?

I know a woman whose husband took his own life. He had threatened her, as well as family members, before turning the gun on himself. It was a horrible time. I was able to spend time with her shortly after the tragedy and was horrified by some of the subtle (and not so subtle) comments that friends and family made to her:

"You need to forgive him."

"Don't be mad at him. He just wasn't himself."

"Keep your voice down. There's no need to get so angry."

I sat, listened, and grieved. Finally, when there was a slight breather, I pulled her aside and said, "You be as angry as you want! If you want to yell, yell! If you want to ask questions, ask questions! If you want to wail and tear your clothes and ask why, why, why!? go ahead. I will be right here by you. Nothing you say is going to offend me, and nothing you do is going to make me question your love for God or the love you had for your husband."

God can take your anger. So write him a letter. Speak aloud to him. Tell him what's on your mind, how you feel about him.

And after all the emotions and feelings are out, dig into the Bible, because it will show you what God is really like. He does care, he can intervene, and he is in control. The Bible won't necessarily answer all your whys, but it will help you focus on God, who knows why.

All of us experience tragedy, hard things in our life. But only YOU can decide how you will respond to such events. Will you become bitter and angry at God? Or will you agree to give up control, even of things you don't understand, to God?

That decision will change the course of the rest of your life and your relationships.

10

Girlfriend 9-1-1!

Hey, girls, it's a fact that we can't "do life" on our own.

All of us have hang-ups, whether our-own-fault induced or the came-with-the-help-of-others variety.

Sometimes we just need girlfriends. Not accountability groups. Not finger wagging. But true girlfriends who love us enough just to tell it like it is and have fun along the way too.

I recall the summer of 1974 and my girlfriends on the 800 block of Buchanan Street in Brunswick, Missouri. Thanks to the combined work efforts of Lana and Toni Lybarger, Angie Woolston, Lesa Reichert, and me, a portion of wooded land just behind Terri Strub's house was made suitable for girlfriend fun.

Between intermittent jaunts to Junior's West-End Grocery for grape soda and mind-numbing "don't touch your brakes!" bicycle races careening down The Big Hill, we constructed a humble abode worthy of reality TV status. We had all the amenities a group of 9- and 10-year-old girls could want: a lean-to fashionably covered with leafy branches to protect us from summer rain showers, as well as soft pine needles to sit on; a kitchen area consisting of two five-pound Folgers coffee cans turned upside down with a portion of metal cut and curled upward, making it possible to light a fire beneath and cook on the small, hot surface *(Kudos to the fine instructions given during a 1972 day camp with Brownie Girl Scout troop No. 412.)* We even had a latrine—complete with shower curtain to ensure absolute privacy.

There's never been quite a place like it. All summer long, from 8:00 A.M. until our mothers called us home long after dark, we girls lived and laughed, fought and giggled in that glorious girlfriend retreat. There wasn't a topic off-limits. Cute boys (David Moser, Bill Myers, and Larry Gash respectively), scary dreams, knock-knock jokes, menstrual cramps *(none of us actually had a period, but things were looking extremely promising for Lana)*, and parental grievances were all up for discussion and debate.

During those hot, muggy days, all it took was hearing the sound of Lana bossing Toni, a glimpse of Angie scrunching her nose and pushing her eyeglasses back on her nose, or the aroma of OFF! bug spray emanating from tick-protected Lesa, to assure me everything was right with the world.

Think about the women you enjoy hanging out with most. Where do you go to unload and unwind? Is it at your kitchen table with a cup of hot tea? Speaking on weekends with your free minutes with Sprint or U. S. Cellular? Or perhaps it's Starbucks—bantering back and forth while throwing back hits of toffee-nut latte? Maybe you prefer catching up on things via MSN messenger, or while breaking a sweat on dual treadmills at your local health center *(a thought, I might add, that has never entered my mind until this very writing moment)*.

No matter the place or time, there are few things better in this life than the camaraderie of women. There's something about knowing you're not alone—knowing there's someone who connects with your life, your joys, your screwups, and your thoughts—that simply makes life more bearable. But let's be perfectly clear: It's one thing to be *told* you're not alone, and quite another to *believe* it.

Over the years I've asked friends and family, as well as complete strangers, the following question: "What good are we to one another if we never let anyone know we don't have it all together?"

Think of the women who have helped you through a crisis or loss.

Think of those who said just the right word at just the right time.

Did they allow you to believe their life was perfect, or come across as emotionally or spiritually aloof?

Probably not.

In all likelihood, those women were right there with you, identifying with your pain and doubt—offering in a very real and tangible fashion the comfort of God. In fact, that's one of the cardinal rules of redemption—"He [God] comes alongside us when we go through hard times, and before you know it, he brings us alongside someone else who is going through hard times so that we can be there for that person just as God was there for us."[1]

The last thing I want or need when facing marital trouble, spiritual apathy, or irrational fear and anxiety is someone telling me why I shouldn't feel the way I do and then giving me tips for getting over it. No, I need to know they have been where I am—if only a bit.

This is why I believe that it's imperative we live and speak authentically before one another. But realizing authentic living almost always entails risk.

If you've already read *Scandalous Grace,* you may recall a chapter titled "The Other Woman."

In it I tell of meeting a drop-dead-gorgeous woman named Cynthia. Within a matter of seconds I had pegged her as some-one having a perfect life, and I couldn't even imagine getting to know her—let alone actually *liking* her. But God has a funny way of drop-kicking women into our life to bring about his purposes.

DROPKICK #1

Cynthia and I were in attendance at a brunch in the summer of 2001. After the meal and shared conversations of some 75 women, we closed the meeting with corporate prayer. As woman after woman prayed aloud, I clearly sensed God direct-ing me to stand up, to walk across the room to where Cynthia was, and to pray for her.

Now remember, ladies: This is Cynthia of blonde hair, svelte figure, and "I don't want to get to know her because she makes me feel insecure" fame. Of course God would ask me to pray for her. But here's the deal: There was actually a bit more detail in regards to the heavenly directive. I didn't put those details in *Scandalous Grace* because, quite honestly, they sounded goofy—wacky—um, weird.

Since then my thinking has changed. I'll tell you why in a

minute. But here goes . . . I not only sensed God telling me to pray for hcr but specifically instructing, *Place your hand on her thigh and pray for her.*

Uh, huh, I told you it was going to sound weird.

Now, despite my stealthy sinner ways, I have been known to obey divine promptings. So this time I stood up. I scanned the room and spotted her kneeling on the floor about 18 feet from me. Making my way around a banquet table and weaving through chairs and other women, I knelt quietly beside her and gently *(you don't even know how gently)* placed my right hand lightly *(fingertips really)* on . . . well, her outer thigh.

Amazingly enough, she didn't slap me.

In fact, after a few seconds of continued silent prayer she slipped her hand over mine and gave it a gentle squeeze as if to say, *I'm glad you're here beside me.* A few minutes later we found ourselves talking and laughing.

Out of that rather odd moment Cynthia and I have somehow forged quite a friendship. She has turned out to be one of the few women in my adult life whom I have trusted with my "I've never told anyone this before" secrets.

However, getting to that point has been neither easy nor comfortable.

DROPKICK #2

About two years into our friendship, during one of our weekly Monday morning phone calls, Cynthia asked a few probing questions regarding one of my many issues. Like many of you, perhaps, I had *alluded* to the problem but had never had the courage to actually blurt out the truth and say, "This is the current mess I'm in, and I'm horribly and shamefully powerless to handle it." I have a hard time admitting I can't control or handle anything . . . thus the need for stealthy communications and such.

So Cynthia, being the friend she is, listened to my further feeble attempts at waffling around the truth.

Then, over the phone line, I heard her take a deep breath.

Silence reigned for a minute before she asked, "Julie, are you telling me everything about this problem?"

My body froze. With eyes darting to and fro, I said, "Well, um, of course, I am."

Again the phone line was dead silent *(my worst nightmare)*.

And then she said, "Julie, you're lying to me."

Busted.

I've never had anyone, let alone a girlfriend, see through my song and dance and actually call me on it. And I didn't like it one bit. In fact, I was a bit miffed that she would even suggest I wasn't being completely forthcoming. *(She was right—I wasn't being completely forthcoming.)* So I did what I do well—I pouted a bit. When I finally opened my mouth to speak, she added the following, "Julie, you're going to have to decide whether you want this friendship to be built upon truth or lies."

So I thought about it.

Did I really want to trust Cynthia with the truth, the whole truth, and nothing but the truth?

Was I willing to let her see the dark side of my life? Was *I* even willing to admit it? And what if she decided she couldn't handle what I told her? Would she hang up and never call back?

Or withdraw in the cold, methodical manner that has iced more than a few of my past friendships?

Tough questions.

Big risks.

The seconds ticked by as I considered my next move. (*This would be a perfect time to add the following: Cynthia is totally comfortable with silence; I, on the other hand, nearly break out in hives if there's a lull of eight seconds or more in a conversation. Cynthia has a double masters in theology and counseling. She's worked on staff with the Minirth-Meyer clinics and knows a thing or two about listening, being comfortable with silence, and boldly—yet lovingly—confronting women who like to sidestep all of the three.*)

Finally I decided, *Why not?*

Why not tell her everything in all its unedited horror?

Taking a deep breath and silently asking God to help me speak truth, I admitted, "I did lie. Here are all the details." And then I told her my secrets—all of them. For once in my life, as an adult woman, I owned up verbally about *everything* to a living, breathing person. Up until that point I had filled journals with my ups and downs, prayed to God on a pretty routine basis, and participated in accountability groups galore. But rarely *(with the exception of my friend Audrey from college)* had I trusted anyone with the details of my sins and struggles.

I probably told Cynthia more than she wanted to know, but with each secret I exposed I began to feel more and more real. Finally I was allowing someone to know the worst (and most vulnerable) things about me! Finally I was stepping out of stealth mode. It felt wonderful.

Over the course of that year Cynthia and I both called upon the other to stand strong when the other was weak and to make up what was lacking in each other's faith.[2] I honestly don't know what we would have done without each other. Despite our being separated by hundreds of miles and the responsibilities of our individual homes and families, we some-how managed to be *there* for each other.

After one particular experience, Cynthia called and asked if I had ever read or studied much about the Old Testament account regarding an angel and a man named Jacob.[3] I hadn't. She went on to tell me a few facts and details, her voice growing more animated as she explained the Middle Eastern culture during the time of Jacob and how men, as well as God, symbolized making a covenant relationship with one another.

"Julie, this is all so amazing," she explained excitedly. "When men made a covenant (a promise or a contract entered into between two or more persons) regarding matters during the time of Jacob, it was common for them to lay their hand on a specific area of the body. You want to guess which region that might be?"

I erupted in laughter and shouted, "Get out!" Then I asked, "Are you serious—is it the thigh?"

"Yep, girlfriend, it is the thigh." Then Cynthia went on to say, "Julie, I believe God made a covenant between you and me the day you sensed him telling you to walk across the room, place your hand on my thigh, and pray for me. I don't want you ever to be embarrassed to tell the *specific* details of that moment."

While I sat there, the power and symbolism of that covenant truly began to sink in. I asked her, "What do you think would have happened if I had not walked over to you that day in the meeting? What would have happened if you had not called me a liar and challenged me to risk rejection by speaking truth?" And then I gasped in amazement. "Cynthia, how different our lives would be without one another!"

And that's only one miniscule glimpse of radical redemption.

It is beyond anything we can imagine or manipulate. It is completely "Other" as Philip Yancey writes in his book, *Rumors of Another World.* It is a noun—the release or rescue from bondage. And it is also a verb—the active choice we make each and every day toward ourselves, God, and those around us. It's also the story of countless girlfriends who so graciously told me of their "always been there" friend.

✳ Let me tell you about my friend Robin. She is a kind and selfless person who has always been there to lend me an ear. When I first started getting so angry at home, I would call her and she would encourage me. She even mentioned she struggled with the same problem. It was so good to know I wasn't alone.

✳ My dear cousin April has always been there for me. Two years ago I had a miscarriage and two weeks after the miscarriage I fell down the stairs and severely hurt my ankle. I was unable to move, feeling depressed, and totally hopeless. April showed up at my door unannounced with her two daughters and a bag of groceries. They cleaned my house, played with my two small children, did my laundry, and made dinner. She saved me!

✳ My girlfriend Tessa agreed to take care of me after I had to have some surgery until my husband got home. Well, it turned out I was allergic to the anesthesia and I ended up "going" from every end. Did she leave? No way! She was there all the way.

✳ I tend to put up walls, especially when going through a painful experience. So many people don't even know something is wrong because I hide it so well. My dearest friend, Tiffany, is always there for me and lets me cry or question or think out loud.

✳ My friend Diana has always been there for me. She guided me through a very difficult time when my integrity and intentions were being misrepresented and misjudged. She was brutally honest in how I had contributed to the misunderstanding and also incredibly wise in advising me and the leaders involved. She knows my love language is acts of service, and she surprised me by painting a room in my house. I always know she's just a phone call away. I love her dearly.

Do you see how God uses these women in our life to rescue us, restore us, and to renovate our heart, mind, spirit, soul, and body? Aren't you thankful for the divine love of God that filters through the hands and feet, words and touch, of women we have come to love and trust?

✳ I have an aunt who has always been there for me. She lives far away, but it doesn't matter. She took me in when I needed to get away from my parents when I was in high school. She loved me. Took care of me. And has been wonderful to me.

✳ One woman comes to mind: Sue Anne. She will come running and have her arms full of food to serve me and my family. This woman left work one day and brought chicken soup to my house when I was sick. She took care of me and my baby all day. She never complained or groaned. She simply loved me at my weakest. And I will never forget what she did nor be able to tell her enough how thankful I am for her in my life.

✳ My mother was always there for me. She died a few years ago but metaphorically speaking she is still with me. She is the reason I became a Christian, because she told me about Jesus. But more than that she "showed" me Jesus when she forgave me time and time again. She was my rock and constant encourager.

✳ I have a friend I see once a year even though we live fairly close together. The best aspect of our friendship is that we always speak at least once a month for an hour. During that time you would never know that we had not seen or spoken to each other since the last conversation. I can always count on her for anything. If I called her right now, she'd come right over.

✳ My sister is my radical girlfriend! We have always been close and we can talk about anything, knowing the other will give biblical advice and encouragement. She challenges me as she shows unconditional love and forgiveness.

✳ My mother has been my "always" girlfriend. She is sarcastic, funny, strong, and lets me talk about anything and everything. She has never hesitated to support me, even when that means telling me she thinks I'm wrong.

✳ Staci has been there for me for over 12 years. My family members are very dysfunctional and they stress me out big-time! I can call her and unload about anything (really, anything) and she will listen nonjudgmentally and give me feedback.

✳ I have a girlfriend who shared a portion of her inheritance with me. Is that like Jesus or what?!

Indeed! That is just like Jesus.[4]

These relationships are part of God's redemptive work in our life. He increases our love, our faith, our trust, and our willingness to step out of our comfort zones, through the love, faith, trust, and willingness to be real, with our friends—with our girlfriends. And one of the things he loves to do is bring us in touch with someone who has been where we have . . . and lived to say, *You can make it through too.*

✳ My girlfriend Amelia knows what it's like to hate someone. She was raped as a college student and ended up quitting school as a result. She blamed that person for all the bad things in her life. She wished him dead and almost killed herself. But then somebody told her about a man named Jesus. She was 32 years old when she asked Jesus to forgive her sins and 33 when she wrote me and said she had forgiven the man who raped her.

She wrote me because my son had been killed by a teenage girl (ran a stoplight while fiddling with her radio) and I was filled with hurt, bitterness, and hate. I prayed the girl would die. And I told everyone; my mother, my priest, the lady at Wal-Mart, and my friend Amelia, that I would never forgive that stupid 17-year-old girl.

Amelia listened to me rant. She held me when I cried so hard I made myself vomit. And she gently and lovingly prayed (I didn't even know it most of the time) that I would see how the hate was killing me.

This went on for close to eight years until one day I simply grew tired of hating. I was too tired to do it. And I wanted (for the first time since my son died) to feel something other than the hate.

Amelia listened to me that day and told me about Jesus. She told me how he had forgiven her of her sin. She told me how much he loved me and how he wanted to wipe clean my heart, my soul, my mind, my thoughts, and my words.

I was ready. While Amelia held my hands, I prayed and asked Jesus to do just that. And he did. I don't think I would have ever made that decision if it hadn't been for my girlfriend Amelia.

✳ I can't have children. My sister Darlene can't have children either. She has been my best friend, as well as my spiritual support through this. She knows what it's like to literally ache in your womb. I love her.

✳ My friend redeemed my life when I was going through a divorce. She knows what it's like to go through one too. And she never preached to me or told me what I should or shouldn't feel. She simply stayed by my side.

So you see, we all live in scorched areas. And according to the research, they're all the same. That means *other women*—some you may know already and some you may meet, as I did Cynthia—are in the same boat with you. They may struggle with varying degrees in each area, but together you're already bonded.

So, girlfriend, go out there and find a girlfriend. Even one will do for now.

Then risk being real.

Falling Forward

 have a 14-year-old son who has enjoyed jumping, climbing, roughhousing, running, swinging, and any other activity ending in "ing" since the moment he discovered he could move. He was a trapeze artist in the womb. At age two-and-a-half, he rode his two-wheel bike sans training wheels over a three-foot retaining wall and landed on a concrete sidewalk. As a nine-year-old he jumped from a 20-foot-high rock cliff *(against his mother's protests, thank you very much)* and came "this" close to striking his head against those same sharp rocks as he fell. Instead he landed flat on his back and scared me nearly speechless. *(I had a few choice words for his father, who was supposedly watching the boy.)*

It didn't take me long, as the mother of a rambunctious son, to learn to be prepared for his inevitable falls. I stocked my bathroom cabinet with Band-Aids, hydrogen peroxide, antibiotic ointments, varied sizes of wound dressings, as well as butterfly Band-Aids and numerous copies of the phone number of our faithful physician, Dr. Keith Peachey.

Each sport my son participates in brings its own unique

aches and pain. Jammed fingers and oozing "strawberries" on the thigh and knee proclaim that it's indeed baseball season. Aching tendons and muscle cramps spell basketball. And crusted scabs on his knees, elbows, and the palms of his hands let me know it's summertime and the season of Rollerblading and skateboarding. But one of the funny things is this . . . Ricky is seldom as bruised or scabbed as some other boys I know. And you know why that is?

It's because the boy isn't afraid to fall.

You can see it in his eyes the moment he snaps down those skates or hops on a board. He expects to fall. He's ready for the fall. And when it happens . . . well, he hops right back up and goes at it again.

Now, ladies, despite appearances to the contrary, there are quite a number of sure things in this crazy thing we call life: the rising and setting of the sun, ocean tides, embarrassing toe-nail fungus, political scandals, laugh *(and worry)* lines, too many stories of Hollywood excess, stubborn soap scum, our children's ability to repeat words and produce bodily gases at highly inopportune moments, and the near mystical certainty that at any given moment in the universe an episode of *Law & Order* is being aired.

Oh, and there's one more . . . the sheer certainty that you and I will sin and fail again on this journey of radical redemption.

In other words, we are going to fall.

Expect it. Don't be surprised. You *will* sin, you *will* fall short. And when *(note that I didn't say "if")* it happens, lean into the Cross. Lean into Jesus—and fall forward.

Really! Fall forward!

Contrary to our usual thinking, not all falling is bad. And falling forward is far different from falling backward. When you fall forward, you can at least see where you're going—even if your nose does get a little bruised on the way down. But when you fall forward with God, you fall directly into his arms—instead of on your backside.

But so often we try to do it all ourselves and end up on our backside. We miss the comforting presence of God's arms around us. If only, like Ricky and his skateboard, we could get over our fear of falling, we would be able to walk more smoothly over the rocks and weeds on life's path. And when we did end up falling, we would experience not only the lavish richness of God's scandalous grace but the healing touch of his radical forgiveness. Then we could get up from our fall just that much quicker, and begin walking with Jesus again.

Now, am I saying you should go out and do something really bad? That you should sin in a big way so you'll know personally what it feels like to be redeemed back from the very pit? Am I taking back everything I've written in chapters 1 through 10? Of course not! But what I want to point out is that many of us continue to punish ourselves for falling—for messing up. For sinning again, after we so much wanted not to. Boy, was the saintly Paul (who considered himself the worst of sinners) right—we continue to do what we don't want to do!

Falling is as sure as our human nature. It will be a part of life as long as we are on this earth. *(Now doesn't that make heaven sound even better? We won't even have the opportunity to mess up because our very nature will be changed. Boy, am I ready!)*

But you and I both know that oftentimes the hardest person

to stop punishing is yourself. *(We women know how to do guilt, recrimination, and angst. We're pros.)*

You may understand that God's forgiven you. But you still know something isn't quite right. You may still feel "dirty" inside. You don't *feel* forgiven.

But *feeling* forgiven has nothing to do with actually *being* forgiven. Verse after verse in the Bible claims that God forgives us when we ask. Yet we still have that tug on our gut when we think about what we've done in the past, even if it's way back in our history. It could be something as "little" as saying something mean to another child in kindergarten. It could be the guilt of "backseat" sexual experimentation while you were a teenager. It could be a lie that you told a coworker. It could be never saying "I love you" to a parent or sibling before that car accident.

Whatever your tug on your gut, realize that the tug is really your disappointment in yourself. That, surprise of surprises, you're not perfect! And you will fail sometimes. But if you expect that human state, rather than being surprised by it, your train won't be derailed.

✳　✳　✳

Somehow we've also fallen into the thinking that the greater the sin, the lesser God's ability to forgive us. And the less we deserve to be forgiven.

But the infinite truth is that Jesus already paid it all. The price for all our sins has been taken care of and there are no exceptions.

So if we accept God's forgiveness, extended through his Son, Jesus Christ, there's no need to fall into Satan's mind-game traps:

MIND GAME #1

If only. . .

GOD'S TRUTH

There's no need for the *Oh, what have I done?* internal speech. Or the *If only I hadn't . . .* refrain. Those nasty little replays of your sins are something Satan uses to keep you discouraged, downtrodden. To keep the blinders on so you can't see the magnificent proportions of my scandalous grace, my radical redemption, or catch a glimpse of the exquisite hope of heaven to come.

Friend, Satan is working a number on you. Don't fall for it!

MIND GAME #2

I'm such a failure. . . .

GOD'S TRUTH

Why continue heaping mud and ashes on your head? I created you, I love you, and I know how fallible you are.

We need not berate ourselves: Look at what I've done now! God will never listen to my prayers.

MIND GAME #3

I'll just do X . . .

GOD'S TRUTH

You can never be "good enough" by yourself. That's why I created a magnificent plan. You need only accept it!

Why is it that we try to "make up" for what we've done—

by working harder, attending church longer, doing more "ministry," or denying ourselves good things because we don't deserve them? We could spend our entire lifetime trying to pay back that debt, and it would still be impossible. And, to be honest, it's more than silly to try to pay for something that's already been paid—in fact, gloriously prepaid by Jesus' death two thousand years ago.

When we work hard to pay the debt, it's as though we're saying, *Well, God, I guess you can't do it alone. You need my help.*

Uh, I don't think so.

The truth is, God doesn't need our help. But we need his! Since we know we will most likely fall (even in those areas where we're trying so hard not to do so, to mend our ways), we must *prepare* to fall. And that means knowing the terrain around us (being aware of Satan's sneaky little ploys that keep us hopping and in trouble). If we're prepared, and we realize that we're up against more than we can handle on our own, we won't be taken by surprise.

PROTECTIVE GEAR: TRUTH WITH A CAPITAL T

Thankfully, God doesn't leave us simply to fend for ourselves. As the Ultimate Parent, God the Father has already provided the protective gear we need to survive the inevitable falls of life. And he has done this willingly and out of love for us as his beloved daughters. One of the best questions ever posed by Jesus spoke to this form of parental love. "If your child asks for bread, do you trick him with sawdust? If he asks for fish, do you scare him with a live snake on his plate? As bad as you are *(and every one of you has heard my horror stories),* you wouldn't think

of such a thing. You're at least decent to your own children.
So don't you think the God who conceived you in love will be
even better?"[1]

One of the best ways God helps us is by revealing through
his Word the protective gear we can use to cover our tender
areas and keep us from harm. God is strong, and he wants you
to develop strength too. "So take everything the Master has set
out for you, well-made weapons of the best materials. And put
them to use so you will be able to stand up to everything the
Devil throws your way."[2] "Take all the help you can get, every
weapon God has issued, so that when it's all over but the shout-
ing you'll still be on your feet."[3]

God knows better than anyone how to protect those he loves.
Consider the "padding" that protects you against the bumps
and lumps of falling as you sometimes skate, other times barely
crawl, along the road of radical forgiveness: Truth.

The New American Standard translation of Ephesians 6:14
reads, "Stand firm therefore, having girded your loins with
truth." Now, I know what a girdle is *(awful, nasty, confining
undergarment that it is . . . but it does do wonders on the tummy,
doesn't it, girls?),* but I'm not quite sure about the meaning of
"girding yourself." So I did a little word study and learned that
to "gird yourself" means to "tie up your loose garments in your
belt." You need to remember that when Paul was writing the
book of Ephesians he was living smack-dab in the middle of
"the Bible days." Men wore robes, togas, and skirts of various
lengths. So when they had to move quickly or get prepared to
run, they would have to "gird their loins" (i.e., gather the flow-
ing parts of their robe/toga into their belt) to keep from tripping

and stumbling and making fools of themselves. If they did not do this, they would indeed stumble.

Fall.

And should they find themselves being pursued by an enemy—someone or something wishing to do them harm—well, one trip on the hem is all it would take to send a person sprawling to the ground and looking up the length of a nice shining sword. Or the jaws of a predator. Jesus used the same Greek word for girding when he said to his disciples in Luke 12:35, "Be dressed in readiness, and keep your lamps alight" (NASB). To gird your loins is to be ready to move, unhindered, at the slightest moment's notice.

And so Paul instructs us to gird ourselves with truth.

But whose truth? Yours? Mine? The latest spiritual guru hocking his wares on Christian television?

Hmm, I don't think so. As always we must return to the source of truth—the Bible. In a famous scene of history, Pilate, the governor of Judea, asks Jesus, "What is truth?"

Good question. Too bad that Pilate never stayed around to hear the answer. John 18:38 records, "Pilate said to Him, 'What is truth?' And when he had said this, he went out again to the Jews. . . ." (NASB).

Seems rather straightforward to say, but if you want to know what truth is, it's wise to wait for the answer! Doing just that may have saved Pilate a whole lot of trouble in the long run. Psalm 119 (NKJV) clearly tells those who will listen:

"So shall I have an answer for him who reproaches me, for I trust in Your word."—*verse 42*

"**Y**ou are near, O Lord, and all Your commandments are truth."
—*verse 151*

"**T**he entirety of Your word is truth, and every one of Your righteous judgments endures forever."—*verse 160*

God is always truthful. He can't be any other way.

But you and me? Oy vey! You know all about those "I've never" secrets *(not-so-secret anymore)* of mine. If we're living and breathing as humans, then we are prone to lies, insincerity, hypocrisy, unrighteousness, error, and deception. And not only are we not truthful, we do things to the truth and against the truth. We try to twist it to suit our own selfish purposes. Because humankind is not of the truth, we as a group as well as individuals continually do things to the truth and against the truth. For example:[4]

- ✳ Romans 1:25 . . . *exchanged* the truth . . .
- ✳ Romans 2:8 . . . *do not obey* the truth . . .
- ✳ 2 Thessalonians 2:12 . . . *did not believe* the truth . . .
- ✳ 2 Timothy 2:18 . . . *gone astray* from the truth . . .
- ✳ 2 Timothy 3:8 . . . *oppose* the truth . . .
- ✳ 2 Timothy 4:4 . . . *turn away* their ears from the truth . . .
- ✳ James 3:14 . . . *lie against* the truth.

Sigh. And those are just a few of the examples in Scripture. *(Frankly, it was too depressing to search for more. . . .)*

If we're going to survive the falls of living, we're going to have to protect ourselves with the padding of truth in three key areas.

TRUTH AS A LIFESTYLE.

We say what we mean, and we mean what we say.

There is no padding, no second-guessing, no half lies or white lies. Our words and actions are truth. Nothing less.

TRUTH AS A BELIEF SYSTEM.

Jesus is the Way, the Truth, and the Life (John 14:6, NASB).

Note the word *the*. Not *a* way, *a* truth, and *a* life. Jesus is the ONLY way, truth, and life. He is the only means by which we can be redeemed, ransomed, radically forgiven . . . for all eternity.

TRUTH AS A RESPONSE TO THE DECEPTION AROUND US (JAMES 5:12).

Our yes means yes, and our no means no.

No wishy-washy living. No "I can do that here because nobody I know will see me."

No "Well, that won't hurt anybody."

Only a simple question: How would Jesus respond? And what would we do if he was physically sitting beside us at that very moment?

My son Ricky learned quickly that to be a better skater, he had to get over his fear of falling and learn how to fall without getting hurt. He had to wear protective gear to cushion the inevitable falls.

And we need to do the same thing. We need to get over our fear of falling, learn to fall well, and wear protective gear for the times when we will fall. Because with the proper padded gear, if you fall forward or even backwards, your vulnerable places (wrists, elbows, knees) will be cushioned from the impact.

Important note: Even if you learn to fall well, you still can hit your head, so make sure that important piece of your body is protected. It's imperative to wear a helmet, and the blood of Jesus Christ provides the only guaranteed-to-be-crack-free one. See Ephesians 6:17 (NASB): "And take the helmet of salvation. . . . "

So, ladies, if you want the Cliff Notes version *(as I did in college)*, here it is: You are going to fall, so don't fight it when you do. But in order to avoid falls, teach yourself how to regain your balance. Yes, we are imperfect. We fall. But we don't have to just fall down.

We can fall to the Cross.

We can fall into the waiting arms of Jesus.

12

Wide-Open Spaces

*W*hoo-ha! How wonderful—how *radical*—it is that God understands the concept of all-or-nothing thinking! And that, even more, he promises each and every one of us, "I've never quit loving you and never will. Expect love, love, and more love!"[1]

And you can. Just listen to some of the women who are now living free in the wide-open spaces created by the radical forgiveness of God being worked out and implemented in their lives.

* I have forgiven everyone (really!).

* I have forgiven my mother for the verbal and physical abuse in our family.

* I was forgiven for a $1,000 mistake by my employer. No lecture, no frown, no nothing! I was so young at the time, and it made an incredible impact on my life.

* My kids have forgiven me for being awful. They made a beautiful card and picked a bouquet of my favorite

flowers—peonies—and said they loved having me
as their mom.

✳ I finally let go of the hatred I had for my alcoholic father.
As I released him from his past, *I* was the one who truly
found freedom.

✳ I have forgiven my parents for not being there for me and
my siblings when we were growing up.

✳ I forgave God for "taking" two babies from me in the womb.
I no longer blame him—or myself.

✳ I had a nervous breakdown. For so many years after that I
felt so guilty for my inability to take care of my children and
love my husband the way I wanted to. But I just couldn't.
At the time I wasn't capable of doing anything but merely
existing. I don't know exactly how it happened but sometime later (it's hard to pinpoint exactly when), I came to
a place where I looked at myself in the mirror and said,
"I forgive you, Leanne, for being sick." While it may sound
simple and trite to some women, it was a huge turning
point in my life and my home. I am forgiven for my sickness
and failures!

✳ I forgave myself for allowing a young man in my home
who nearly raped me. As my anger toward him diminished,
so did my anger toward myself. I finally realized it wasn't
my fault for trusting him. But it was wrong for me to choose
to hate.

✳ I forgave my dad six years ago. He always talked down to me when I was a teen. He even told me once that I wasn't good enough to be his daughter. That hurt went deep. But I finally let the ache and the pain go. Now I really do love my dad. I know he did the best he could do, considering the way he was raised as a child.

✳ An ex-boyfriend of mine forgave me for aborting the baby he fathered.

✳ My friend forgave me for sharing a secret she told me with another friend.

✳ I have forgiven my husband for incurring over $6,000 in debt that he had hidden from me for close to three years. I had no other choice. This man has loved me and forgiven so many ugly things about me. We are a team, and I was determined to show him the same grace and mercy he has demonstrated to me time and time again.

✳ When I was 11 years old, my adopted father sexually abused me. It continued for two years. At 19 I met my husband. Thankfully, he is nothing like my father. When my youngest son was born, I saw my father with new eyes. I realized he is a broken, sinful man. Just like my husband. Just like me. I chose to forgive him at that moment. Yes, I have put up certain boundaries because of his sin, but I can truly say I have forgiven him for those things.

✳ I have recently, through the help of a Beth Moore Bible study, been able to forgive myself for the hurt I had caused my children. I also forgave my dad for leaving my mom and my siblings when I was 16 years old.

✳ My family went through a particularly bad time three years ago: two miscarriages, my husband in the hospital for four days with an infection in his system that the doctors could not pinpoint, and a daughter who was losing a battle with anorexia. It seemed like the only two emotions I had for God during that time were pain and betrayal. I didn't understand why he let one bad thing after another happen. Well, now that I'm a bit further down the road I can tell you that it still takes a lot of effort to stay away from the bad spots (doubting God, frustration with my daughter, questioning why, why, why?). But I can also honestly tell you that God has forgiven me for my lack of trust and faith. Every day he seems to give me enough for that day. I'm not perfect, and yet God loves me! And that's enough for today.

✳ At age 27 I realized I'll never have certain things come true in my life. And I looked back on some of my choices and asked God to forgive me for not asking him what the best thing to do was. I'm married to a man who does not believe in God, and some of the things I feel most "empty" about are a result of that choice. But I know God has forgiven me, and I know every day he is helping me to love my husband in a way that draws him to the truth of Jesus.

✳ I watched my father die a very painful death. I begged and pleaded with God to take away his pain . . . and God didn't. So I despised God for years. Why would I want to follow someone who did so little, if anything, to help?

Then I found a letter my father had written me before the pain became too great for him to hold a pen. He told me things about his past. He told me secret sins he had carried with him up until that moment. He told me to look past what may lie ahead for him and to consider all the things he had taught me as a young child about Jesus.

That letter changed my life. Out of respect for my father I began to mull over things. I read my Bible a time or two. And I made an appointment with the pastor of my father's church and let him know how angry I was at God. Instead of judging me or lecturing me, the pastor simply listened. He said very little. But when I left that day, I seemed able really to believe God might be someone I needed—and wanted—to know after all.

Well, it's two years later, and I took the plunge! I asked for forgiveness of all my sin (you don't know what a work of redemption this is!), and I no longer hold a grudge against God. I am free. And the best thing about it is this: Someday I'm going to see my dad. I hope Jesus told him I read that letter!

Now this is living, girls!

This is what radical forgiveness is all about!

Being able to throw off everything that has tied you down. Everything that has worked against you, wiggled its way into your soul and into your thought life. Everything that has convinced you that God is through with you. That you are worthless—of no value to God, others, or yourself.

And then there's the magenta hue of Radical Forgiveness that splashes so boldly across our life.

✳ ✳ ✳

Forgiveness opens a new world of possibilities. It frees us so we no longer have anything to hide!

Think of it, girlfriends!

No secrets.

No *if-onlys.*

No *what-ifs.*

No *I wish I'ds* . . .

No *I wish I hadn'ts* . . .

Nothing to fear, and nothing to be ashamed of either. We can rest at night, as well as face the morning with a clear conscience and a fresh start, no matter what happened yesterday.

Scandalous grace reveals that no one is beyond God, beyond hope.

Radical forgiveness upends our life, showing us that we can choose to live in a radically different way.

And then, at long last, without the clouds hovering over us that have been dimming our vision, we are able to see clearly what lies ahead. Instead of looking down at ourselves, our shame, fear, or guilt . . . instead of focusing on our traumas and sins . . . instead of narrowing our eyes in hate and anger at those who have hurt us . . . we are free to lift our eyes.

What do we see there, in the beautiful blue sky? A glimpse of the horizon—and the *exquisite hope* of heaven!

May the radical forgiveness offered through Jesus Christ envelop your life in every way . . .

Enveloping Forgiveness . . .
covering all your sins.

Enveloping Forgiveness . . .
surrounding your days and nights with peace.

Enveloping Forgiveness . . .
sheltering you in the close protection of his arms.

Enveloping Forgiveness . . .
protecting you from the enemy.

Enveloping Forgiveness . . .
harboring you safe forevermore.

Enveloping Forgiveness . . .
guarding your heart and life with truth.

Enveloping Forgiveness . . .
providing sanctuary for your soul.

Forgiveness Observed

These quotes have acted as stepping-stones on my own journey toward understanding God's radical forgiveness. Perhaps they'll do the same for you.

A true Christian is a sign of contradiction—a living symbol of the Cross. He or she is a person who believes the unbelievable, bears the unbearable, forgives the unforgivable, loves the unlovable, is perfectly happy not to be perfect, is willing to give up his or her will, becomes weak to be strong . . . and finds love by giving it away.
JOSEPH ROY, *Leadership, Vol. 5, no. 4.*

And he did it, rescued us from certain doom. And he'll do it again, rescuing us as many times as we need rescuing.
2 CORINTHIANS 1:10, *The Message, 2095.*

Forgiving does not erase the bitter past. A healed memory is not a deleted memory. Instead, forgiving what we cannot forget creates a new way to remember. We change the memory of our past into a hope for our future.
LEWIS B. SMEDES, *quoted on http://www.christianitytoday.com/ct/2002/149/ 55.0html. The quote is from "Forgiveness—The Power to Change the Past," an article that originally appeared in the January 7, 1983, issue of Christianity Today.*

If we could read the secret history of our enemies, we would find in each person's life sorrow and suffering enough to disarm all hostility. **HENRY WADSWORTH LONGFELLOW**

Forgiveness does not change the past, but it does enlarge the future. **HARRIET BEECHER STOWE**

Whoever approaches Me walking, I will come to him running; and he who meets Me with sins equivalent to the whole world, I will greet him with forgiveness equal to it. **E. W. HOWE**

In Him we have redemption through His blood, the forgiveness of our trespasses, according to the riches of His grace. **EPHESIANS 1:7 (NASB)**

We all agree that forgiveness is a beautiful idea until we have to practice it. **C. S. LEWIS,** quoted in Draper's Book of Quotations for the Christian World, edited by Edythe Draper (Wheaton: Tyndale House Publishers, Inc., 1992), Entry 4104.

Forgiveness is the scent that the rose leaves on the heel that crushes it. **MARK TWAIN**

At some point you pardon the people in your family for being stuck together in all their weirdness, and when you can do that, you can learn to pardon everyone. **ANNE LAMOTT,** Traveling Mercies

It is for freedom that Christ has set us free. Stand firm, then, and do not let yourself be burdened again by a yoke of slavery. **GALATIANS 5:1 (NIV)**

Everyone says forgiveness is a lovely idea, until they have someone to forgive. . . . I am telling you what Christianity is. I did not invent it. And there, right in the middle of it, I find "Forgive us our sins as we forgive those that sin against us." There is no slightest suggestion that we are offered forgiveness on any other terms. It is made perfectly clear that if we do not forgive we shall not be forgiven. There are no two ways about it.   **C. S. LEWIS,** *Mere Christianity*

Clara Barton was never known to hold resentment against anyone. One time a friend recalled to her a cruel thing that had happened to her some years previously, but Clara seemed not to remember the incident. "Don't you remember the wrong that was done you?" the friend asked Clara. She answered calmly, "No, I distinctly remember forgetting that."
JAMES S. HEWETT, *Illustrations Unlimited* (Wheaton: Tyndale House Publishers, Inc., 1988), 216.

I've tried everything and nothing helps. I'm at the end of my rope. Is there no one who can do anything for me? Isn't that the real question?
ROMANS 7:24, *The Message*, 2044.

The church cannot set false borders on grace. There are no limits on divine mercy toward penitent people. There are no boundaries on forgiveness. The church must discipline sin in its midst, but we cannot deny a penitent person, no matter how serious his sin may have been. Someone might protest, "But we want to make sure he will never do it again." We cannot have that assurance. If he sins seventy times seven, we must forgive him that many times. Refusing to forgive is a sin, a sin that is doubly destructive to Christian joy, because it not only steals the original offender's joy, but it also diminishes the joy of the one who is refusing to forgive. Failure to forgive . . . is an extremely destructive kind of sin.
JOHN MACARTHUR, *The Freedom and Power of Forgiveness*

Now, regarding the one who started all this—the person in question who caused all this pain—I want you to know that I am not the one injured in this as much as, with a few exceptions, all of you. So I don't want to come down too hard. What the majority of you agreed to as punishment is punishment enough. Now is the time to forgive this man and help him back on his feet. If all you do is pour on the guilt, you could very well drown him in it. My counsel now is to pour on the love.

The focus of my letter wasn't on punishing the offender but on getting you to take responsibility for the health of the church. So if you forgive him, I forgive him. Don't think I'm carrying around a list of personal grudges. The fact is that I'm joining in with *your* forgiveness, as Christ is with us, guiding us. After all, we don't want to unwittingly give Satan an opening for yet more mischief—we're not oblivious to his sly ways! **2 CORINTHIANS 2:5-11,** *The Message, 2097.*

Conversion begins with turning, and forgiveness invites that turning. For most people, the experience of God's forgiveness occurs most directly through the forgiveness of their brothers and sisters. Only out of that forgiveness are people enabled to move from their past into God's future for their lives. **JIM WALLIS**

Forgiveness is the final form of love. **REINHOLD NIEBUHR**

You will know that forgiveness has begun when you recall those who hurt you and feel the power to wish them well. **LEWIS B. SMEDES**

Let us always keep in mind that the first word from the cross was a word of forgiveness!
ROBERT C. SHANNON, 1000 *Windows (Cincinnati, Ohio: Standard Publishing Company, 1997).*

Ronald Reagan's attitude after the 1982 attempt on his life made an impression on his daughter, Patti Davis: "The following day my father said he knew his physical healing was directly dependent on his ability to forgive John Hinckley. By showing me that forgiveness is the key to everything, including physical health and healing, he gave me an example of Christ-like thinking."

TAKEN FROM *ANGELS DON'T DIE.* *Fresh Illustrations for Preaching & Teaching (Baker), from the editors of Leadership.*

Percentage of Americans who pray to forgive others: 86 percent. Who pray for forgiveness for themselves: 92 percent. **GALLUP POLL**

A guy complained to his buddy that whenever he argued with his wife, she got historical. His friend said, "You mean hysterical." He said, "No, historical. She dredges up the past and reminds me of every time I've failed her in the past." **ONLINE QUOTE**

On February 9, 1960, Adolph Coors III was kidnapped and held for ransom. Seven months later his body was found on a remote hillside. He had been shot to death. Adolph Coors IV, then fifteen years old, lost not only his father but his best friend. For years young Coors hated Joseph Corbett, the man who was sentenced to life for the slaying. Then in 1975 Ad Coors became a Christian. While he divested himself of his interest in the family beer business, he could not divest himself of the hatred that consumed him. Resentment seethed within him and blighted his growth in faith. He prayed to God for help because he realized how his hatred for Corbett was alienating him from God and other persons. The day came, however, when claiming the Spirit's presence, Ad Coors visited the maximum security unit of Colorado's Canon City penitentiary and tried to talk with Corbett. Corbett refused to see him. Coors left a Bible inscribed with

this message: "I'm here to see you today and I'm sorry that we could not meet. As a Christian I am summoned by our Lord and Savior, Jesus Christ, to forgive. I do forgive you, and I ask you to forgive me for the hatred I've held in my heart for you." Later Coors confessed, "I have a love for that man that only Jesus Christ could have put in my heart."
JAMES S. HEWETT, *Illustrations Unlimited* (Wheaton: Tyndale House Publishers, Inc., 1988), 215.

Every part of Scripture is God-breathed and useful one way or another—showing us truth, exposing our rebellion, correcting our mistakes, training us to live God's way.
2 TIMOTHY 3:16, *The Message*, 2172.

If you wish to travel far and fast, travel light. Take off all your envies, jealousies, unforgiveness, selfishness, and fears. **GLENN CLARK**

When you forgive you in no way change the past—but you sure do change the future.
BERNARD MELTZER, *quoted in Draper's Book of Quotations for the Christian World, edited by Edythe Draper* (Wheaton: Tyndale House Publishers, Inc., 1992), Entry 4108.

A Radical Recipe

This easy, chocolatey treat is guaranteed to cure any PMS or otherwise craving* . . . you can worry about the calories later!

DIVINE DOUBLE CHOCOLATE-CHIP COOKIES
Beat with electric mixer until creamy:

> **1 cup butter**
> **$\frac{2}{3}$ cup white sugar**
> **$\frac{2}{3}$ cup brown sugar**
> **1 tsp. vanilla**
> **2 eggs**

Then add:

> **2 cups flour**
> **$\frac{3}{4}$ cup baking cocoa**
> **1 tsp. baking soda**
> **$\frac{1}{2}$ tsp. salt**

Beat until creamy again. Stir in 2 cups chocolate chips.* Drop by spoonfuls (or use cookie scoop) onto ungreased cookie sheets.

Bake at 350 degrees for 9-11 minutes until firm. Let stand for 2 minutes. Remove to wire racks to cool completely.

*If you only want a few cookies to tempt you at a time, or want to use this as an easy pull-from-the-freezer dessert, here's a handy hint: Drop by spoonfuls (or use cookie scoop) into a pan (that will fit in your freezer) lined with wax paper. Freeze until firm (hint: don't freeze more than one layer of cookie balls at a time or they'll stick together). Place in a plastic bag and label: "Bake at 350 degrees, 9-11 minutes." Place bag in freezer. When ready to bake, take out the number of cookie balls you wish to bake. Let them thaw approximately half an hour or until soft to the touch. Bake and enjoy!

About the Author

Call her a twenty-first-century Erma Bombeck with a pleasantly skewed twist! Julie Ann Barnhill's outrageous humor will indeed have you "laughing so hard you snort" and clapping your hands with glee. With her disarming wit and generous doses of vulnerability and authenticity, both on stage and in print, she's become a best-selling author and popular national speaker.

Julie's first featured book, *She's Gonna Blow! Real Help for Moms Dealing with Anger,* caught the attention of American television and radio producers nationwide, as did *'Til Debt Do Us Part: Real Help for Couples Dealing with Finances,* in Canada and Britain. *Scandalous Grace* has garnered zillions of e-mails. Julie has appeared on such programs as: *Oprah, CNN Sunday Morning,* Dick Clark's *The Other Half,* CNBC's *PowerLunch,* and the Canadian television show *It's a New Day.* Her radio spots include: *National Public Radio, Janet Parshall's America*, the *Midday Connection* in Chicago, and a two-day interview that aired March 17-18, 2003, with radio legend Dr. James Dobson on *Focus on the Family Broadcasting.* Julie is also a contributing editor for *Today's Christian Woman.*

Julie is a spunky, sassy, and thought-provoking speaker. She challenges her audiences to "fasten their seat belts!" as she dispenses the lone antidote for remaining sane amidst life's roller-coaster ride of emotional, financial, physical, and spiritual ups and downs—the medicinal cure of guffaw-inducing, jaw-aching, "my stomach muscles hurt so much" laughter!

She is also the mother of three sometimes annoying, always amusing, challenging, stubborn, funny, and argumentative children. And wife to one hubby who has co-owned her dream of speaking and writing since 1984, the year they met. Amazingly, this man thinks she can do anything. *(Okay, anything but mend clothes. Her motto is: If you lose a button, buy a new shirt. Got a hole in your sock? Go buy a 12-pack.)*

Julie, her husband, and their three dependents live in a small (population 486, including decorative yard dwarfs) village located in western Illinois. In that town people use riding lawn mowers as all-terrain vehicles. In fact, Julie about jumped out of her new-neighbor skin when John Deere and Snapper tractors sputtered to the post-office door! It's a place where entertainment is somewhat limited to pulling up a lawn chair and watching a neighbor trim his 25-foot elm tree with a handsaw and rickety ladder. But it's also the kind of old-fashioned place where your neighbor makes you homemade meatballs in the middle of winter and brings them over "just because."

You can visit Julie Barnhill's Web site at: *www.juliebarnhill.com.*

If you are interested in having Julie Ann Barnhill speak at your special event, please contact her directly at her Web site or at Julie@juliebarnhill.com

Endnotes

1 (http://www.christianitytoday.com/ct/2002/149/55.0.html) This quote is from an article that originally appeared in the January 7, 1983 issue of *Christianity Today*.

CHAPTER TWO: A Mess of Magnificent Proportions
1 James 5:16, Eugene H. Peterson, *The Message* (Colorado Springs: NavPress, 2002), 2208.
2 Ephesians 1:7, ibid., 2126.
3 Romans 5:8, ibid., 2039.
4 Isaiah 43:25, ibid., 1292.
5 Colossians 3:13, ibid., 2148.
6 1 John 3:5-6, ibid., 2226.
7 Romans 5:1, ibid., 2039.
8 Romans 7:24-25, ibid., 2044.

CHAPTER THREE: I've Never Told This to Anyone . . .
1 Proverbs 28:13, *The Message,* 1153.
2 Numbers 32:23, ibid., 287.
3 Romans 8:29, ibid., 2046.
4 Hebrews 12:1, ibid., 2196.
5 John 14:6, ibid., 1950.
6 John 8:44, *New American Standard Bible* (LaHabra, Calif.: The Lockman Foundation, 1977).
7 Job 1:6, *The Message*, 843.

8 Ephesians 2:2, *New American Standard Bible*.

9 2 Corinthians 11:3, *The Message*, 2108.

10 Matthew 13:19, ibid., 1770.

11 John 10:10, ibid., 1940.

12 John 10:28-29, ibid., 1941.

13 Genesis 3:4-5, ibid., 24.

14 Revelation 12:9, ibid., 2251.

15 Proverbs 18:24, ibid., 1130.

16 2 Timothy 2:13, ibid., 2170.

17 Romans 8:39, ibid., 2046.

18 Philippians 4:8, ibid., 2141.

19 Romans 8:38-39, ibid., 2046.

20 James 5:16, ibid., 2208.

CHAPTER FOUR: Déjà Vu . . . All Over Again

1 Ecclesiastes 1:10, *The Message,* 1164.

2 Ecclesiastes 1:9, ibid.

CHAPTER FIVE: It's All about Me

1 Romans 7:15, *The Message,* 2043.

2 Romans 7:19, ibid., 2044.

3 Romans 7:16-17, ibid., 2043.

4 Romans 3:9, ibid., 2035.

5 Psalm 51:5, ibid., 975.

6 Psalms 51:5, *New American Standard Bible*.

7 Romans 5:12, *The Message,* 2040.

8 Galatians 5:17, ibid., 2122.

9 Galatians 5:19-21, ibid., 2122-2123.

10 Romans 7:21, ibid., 2044.

11 Romans 7:23, ibid.

12 Romans 7:25, ibid.

CHAPTER SIX: Trading Spaces

1 Romans 5:15, *The Message,* 2040.

2 Hebrews 7:22, ibid., 2189.

3 Romans 5:15, ibid., 2040.

4 Romans 5:19, ibid., 2040.

5 Reverend Fred R. Bartlett, online sermon, http://www.stdunstans.org/ sermons/fafred/02_03_29_when_i_survey_the_wondrous_cross.htm accessed May 2004.

6 1 John 2:1, *The Message*, 2223.

7 1 John 2:1, *New American Standard Bible*.

8 Hebrews 7:25, ibid.

9 Revelation 3:14, *The Message*, 2241.

10 Hebrews 12:2, *New American Standard Bible*.

11 Hebrews 9:28, ibid.

12 Revelation 1:8, *New King James Bible*.

13 1 John 5:20, *The Message*, 2230.

14 Philippians 3:4-7, ibid., 2140.

15 Philippians 3:8, ibid.

16 Isaiah 52:14, ibid., 1313.

17 Matthew 26:12, ibid., 1798.

18 Luke 23:34, ibid., 1910.

19 Luke 23:43, ibid., 1910.

20 PageWise: We've Got Answers, at http://scsc.essortment.com/ britishcrownje_rvfh.htm accessed May 2004.

21 Revelation 19:16, *The Message*, 2261.

22 Deuteronomy 10:14, ibid., 315.

23 Deuteronomy 10:12-13, ibid., 315.

24 Romans 10:9, ibid., 2049.

25 Romans 10:10, ibid., 2050.

26 Romans 10:9-10, *New American Standard Bible*.

27 1 John 1:9, *The Message*, 2223.

28 Ephesians 1:7, ibid., 2126.

CHAPTER SEVEN: I Would If I Could . . . But I Can't, So I Won't

1 Ephesians 2:8, *New American Standard Bible*.

2 1 Corinthians 1:18, ibid.

3 Acts 15:11, ibid.

4 1 John 2:1, *The Message*, 2223.

5 Colossians 2:8, ibid., 2146.

6 See Romans 8:28.

7 Romans 6:15-18, *The Message,* 2041-2042.

8 Proverbs 13:12, *New American Standard Bible.*

9 http://open-mind.org/Serenity.htm accessed May 2004.

CHAPTER EIGHT: Infinity + 1

1 2 Peter 3:8, *The Message*, 2220.

2 2 Peter 3:9, ibid.

3 Matthew 5:40-42, ibid., 1753.

4 Matthew 6:19-20, ibid., 1755.

5 Matthew 18:12-14, ibid., 1780.

6 Matthew 27:52-53, ibid., 1805.

7 John 3:16, ibid., 1921.

8 Romans 5:10, ibid., 2040.

9 Psalm 103:12, *New American Standard Bible.*

10 Isaiah 43:25, *The Message,* 1292.

11 Isaiah 43:25, *New American Standard Bible.*

12 Hebrews 6:18, *The Message*, 2187.

13 1 John 2:25, *New American Standard Bible.*

14 Romans 7:17-18, *The Message*, 2044.

15 "'Jesusy' Anne Lamott" Agnieszka Tennant, associate editor of *Christianity Today*, http://www.christianitytoday.com/ct/2003/001/8.56.html accessed April 2004. Original interview found in January 21, 2003, *Christianity Today* magazine.

16 1 John 1:9, *The Message,* 2223.

CHAPTER NINE: Forgive and Forget? . . . and Other Myths

1 Dan Allender, "Forgive and Forget and Other Myths of Forgiveness," *Discipleship Journal,* Issue Seventy (1992), 18.

2 Isaiah 55:8-9, *The Message,* 1317.

3 Galatians 6:7, ibid., 2124.

4 1 John 2:12, ibid., 2224.

CHAPTER TEN: Girlfriend 9-1-1!

1 2 Corinthians 1:3-4, *The Message,* 2095.

2 Romans 15:1, ibid., 2059.

3 Genesis 32:25ff, ibid., 71.

4 Hebrews 9:15, ibid., 2191.

CHAPTER ELEVEN: Falling Forward

1 Matthew 7:9-11, *The Message,* 1756.

2 Ephesians 6:10-11, ibid., 2134.

3 Ephesians 6:13, ibid.

4 Material adapted from online information found at: http://
   www.calvarychapel.com/cheyenne/Library/49-Ephesians/
   Ephesians0614a.html accessed April 2004.

CHAPTER TWELVE: Wide-Open Spaces

1 Jeremiah 31:3, *The Message,* 1418.

You've experienced the incredible transformation of
Radical Forgiveness. *Now celebrate the liberating and tantalizing realities of* Scandalous Grace!

Extravagant.
Audacious.
Beyond reasonable limits.
That's God's love for you.
But do you live like it?

Scandalous Grace is the *zing* of encouragement every woman needs to transform her thoughts about herself . . . and change her relationships, for the good. With gutsy honesty and stories that'll have you "laughing so hard you snort," Julie Barnhill reveals how you can live, day by day, in the knowledge of God's unconditional love in the midst of "loose ends."

No matter what your past has been, no matter what dreams have or haven't been fulfilled, and no matter what situation you current- ly face, you can feel, taste, and touch the love of God—*personally!*

ISBN 0-8423-8297-6
Available now at a bookstore near you!

CHECK OUT THESE EXCITING NEW FICTION AUTHORS FROM TYNDALE HOUSE PUBLISHERS!

The newest voices in contemporary fiction bring you stories you will never forget. . . .

SUSAN MAY WARREN

Available Now!

ISBN 0-8423-8117-1, ISBN 0-8423-8118-X, ISBN 0-8423-8119-8

Discover the Deep Haven series, where intrigue, adventure, and romance combine in stories that will touch your heart and stir your soul.

Coming Spring 2005!

ISBN 1-4143-0086-7

Book 1 of the Team Hope search and rescue series. Five friends are bound together by their belief that God's mercies are new every morning. Your heart will be gripped as these heroes put their lives on the line, risking everything for a cause greater than themselves. . . .

RENE GUTTERIDGE

Available Now!

ISBN 0-8423-8602-5

In this first book by best-selling author Rene Gutteridge, FBI special agent Mick Kline is on a quest to solve his brother's murder. Readers will discover that nothing is quite as it seems as Mick searches for a faceless killer whose soul harbors a storm of its own.

Coming Spring 2005!

ISBN 0-8423-8765-X

In the prequel to *The Splitting Storm*, football coach Mick Kline's life is spiraling out of control. Accused of kidnapping a young woman, Mick faces a ruthless district attorney and a wall of condemning evidence. . . .